I0152488

Sprung
Poetry of Emergence

TINA AZARIA

SPRUNG, Poetry of Emergence. Copyright © 2014 Tina Azaria.

All rights reserved.

No part of this book may be used or reproduced in any manner whatsoever without written permission except in the case of brief quotations embodied in critical articles and reviews. For information please contact AlembicArts.com

Poetry / Women Authors

ISBN-10: 0989225801
ISBN-13: 978-0-9892258-0-9

DEDICATION

I dedicate this book with love
to my husband, who has championed my work
since the day we met and to my two beautiful sons -
the greatest teachers I have had.
I dedicate these poems to all future generations.
I am obliged, as one of your ancestors,
to hand you a world worth living in.
May I live to fulfill my obligation.

CONTENTS

SPRUNG

ACKNOWLEDGMENTS

This book would not exist without the ongoing, multifaceted support of my husband Christian who has encouraged this project since its inception. Huge thanks to my awesome sons, Noah and Tobin, who have been my adaptable and inspiring companions throughout this wild journey.

Much love and gratitude to all of my amazing friends who have continually affirmed the validity of this project and have rallied me forward through my doubts and fears. Special thanks to Judith Wonstolen for encouraging my poetic voice early on and to Rebecca Harrell for prompting me to grow into a more responsible steward of the creative works that flow through me.

A big thank you to Sandra Shelley and the countless guides and teachers who have held up signposts along the path. I am unceasingly grateful for everyone and everything that has sustained and informed this project. Finally, I acknowledge my family and my ancestors for bestowing on me the love, strength, and the rich fertile soil in which the seeds of the future grow.

TINA AZARIA

Introduction

Sprung *past of* spring.

[1]**Spring** *vb* \ **sprang** \ **sprung** \ **springing** 1 a : DART, SHOOT (2): to be resilient or elastic: also: to move by elastic force. b: to become warped 2 : to issue with speed and force or as a stream 3 a : to grow as a plant b : to issue by birth or descent c : to come into being : ARISE : d *archaic* : DAWN. 4 a : to make a leap or series of leaps : to leap or jump suddenly : to stretch out in height : RISE : 5 : to bring about or undergo splitting or cracking of: to undergo the opening of: to bend by force : to leap over : 6 : to produce or disclose suddenly or unexpectedly: to make lame : STRAIN : to release or cause to be released from confinement or custody

Sprung rhythm *n* : a poetic rhythm designed to approximate the natural rhythm of speech and characterized by the frequent juxtaposition of single accented syllables and the occurrence of mixed types of feet

I have been unsure how to go about compiling this, my first book of writing and poems. The material found herein spans nearly three decades. The questions arise: why have I waited so long and why now, after all these years, take the time to compile these writings into a book? Many answers abound.

The poems in this book are no more than spontaneous expressions sprung from deep unconscious waters into the well of my pen as I've sat journaling for countless hours over the past thirty-some years. I journal every day. Journaling opens a doorway into deeper regions within my psyche – into my personal unconscious filled with half-remembered and completely cut-off personal material and even further into what I can, thus far, only described as the archetypal realms of the collective unconscious and the realm of the human imagination in all its vastness.

My impulse to write comes from a need to process my thoughts, feelings, and experiences, to express myself, and to tend my relationship to the inner and outer worlds. Creative expression, in many forms, has been an invaluable tool for me, a guiding star on the night sea journey, a flickering light leading me through dark and trying times.

Although creative expression has sprung up naturally in my life, sharing my expressions is another story. It is a place of great vulnerability for me, a place of shadowy fears born of lasting impressions of the darker sides of human nature – the parts that condemn, reject, destroy and devour – as found in myself and others.

It is a sensitive thing to share one's innermost thoughts, well-hidden perceptions, and places of confusion, isolation and wounding. I see my contemporaries attack, criticize and berate the personal voice that whispers and screams in the honest art of others. This world can be a hostile environment for delicate sprouts of creative expression to take root and attempt to survive in. So, it's a vulnerable place to begin with. In addition, as luck would have it, much of my poetic inspiration has developed and proliferated in the compost pile of my life, with all of its rich, life-enhancing rottenness and decay, (as it does for many).

Many of the poems in this collection lack maturity, skill and refinement, but I have chosen to include them anyway. They have been part of the mytho-poetic journey that has fertilized this work. And for me, there's an honesty in including work I'm not entirely proud of. It's a fundamental part of the wholeness I seek to embody and portray.

I have lived from, and therefore write from the perspective of a woman that has been shattered by traumatic events and has undergone the laborious task of piecing myself back together. This is what I've experienced and this is what I've needed to heal through creative expression.

Though I find them to be clumsy at times, modern culture seems to love labels. This has caused me and my work to sometimes become affiliated with feminism. I did not then, nor do I now chose to label myself as any sort of "ist". I do not mind if others choose to label and associate themselves, but I prefer that others do not take it upon themselves to do that for me. The anger that sometimes comes through in my poetry is not philosophical or abstract. It is not meant to be an "ist" statement, though it can be interpreted and has at times been adopted as such. It is simply my raw, lived emotion that needed to be expressed lest it fester and come out in less creative, more destructive ways.

For years, I have withheld from sharing much of the creative work that has arisen from my heart and hands for many complex reasons including the labels and categorizations and the sometimes ruthless opining of a world full of self-proclaimed critics. Although I've seen this book in my mind's eye for well over a decade, Sprung (its name since 2002) has had a life of its own from the very beginning. I've had to trust that these poems would spring out into the world when the right conditions became present, both internally and externally. The time is come. It is springtime. This book has sprung at last.

The decision to finally, irrevocably commit to producing this book came in January 2013, on the heels of a commanding dream. I dreamt I was surrounded by art and piles of writing that I had produced. As I entered the borderland between dreaming and waking, a booming voice instructed: "Go for the low-hanging fruit!" Upon waking, I instinctively sensed the message of the dream. I had recently been hit with a realization (after working through some cavernous psychic material) that it was time to begin sharing, on a much larger scale, the mountains of art and writing I'd been accumulating. Yet I was daunted by the seemingly insurmountable task of sorting, sifting, compiling and packaging it. Where to begin? The dream answered the question simply. "Go for the low-hanging fruit!"

As I contemplated the words, it became quickly apparent that one approach to sharing my work was to begin with pieces that were ripe and ready to pluck – the bounty that requires minimal effort to harvest. It's ridiculously obvious now. Such things usually are, once we finally see them. But at the time it was a revelation.

This book was an idea that had been sitting on a shelf for too long. I had many failed attempts at creating it and gave up many times. Now, it became a clear project of gathering up the low-lying crop. I had historically been overwhelmed by decisions such as which poems to include and how to arrange them. This time, the basic criteria became: Do I have a digital copy of it? Is it a complete work? Can it be published with minimal, or better yet, no editing? If a poem fell into the "yes" category for all of the above, then it went into the pot.

As I was sifting through my poems, I noticed there were certain verses that have a lyrical quality, suggesting musical interpretation may be appropriate. Those poems went into their own pile and have mostly not been included in this book. What does appear in this volume is roughly a third of the poems I've written and managed to input into my computer. I have admittedly been a rather poor steward of my creative musings. Too much of it has been stashed away in boxes, drawers, folders, files, or been scattered throughout dozens of journals, notebooks, and sketchpads. That work doesn't meet the low-hanging criteria. That's a harvesting project for another time.

What is found herein is essentially a basket of the low-hanging fruit of my rough and untrained poetic expression. I intend it to be the first of many. I hope that those who hunger for poetic soul-food may partake of this harvest, draw from it what nourishes them and release any indigestible bits back into the compost of imagination.

I arranged the poems as if they were steps on a journey. The poems, in fact, were derived from trips and strides experienced on my personal passage through this world. I think of them as a kind of footprint in the mud, in the snow, in the sand. They say: "Here is where I have walked…"

By now, perhaps the choice of the title *Sprung* may be obvious. But what about the idea of emergence? Clearly the word "emerge" directly relates to the definition of *spring* and *sprung*. But there's more to it than that. It has to do with the nature of this paradoxical journey, this heavenly and hellish ride I've been on and the idea of divine timing, of cycles, stages, and the timing involved in transformation. The idea of emergence has also been germinating inside me for quite some time.

Emergence: noun: 1 : the process of coming into view or becoming exposed after being concealed 2 : the process of complex pattern formation from more basic constituent parts

My story of emergence begins with the inquiry into why I experienced a very protracted waiting period in publishing this work. The answer began dawning on me one night, in 2008, as I sat in bed reading about the initiation rituals undertaken cross culturally by shamans-in-training. Before one steps into the privileges and responsibilities of dedicating oneself to being a keeper of the dreams, visions, and healing powers of their people - to call oneself a shaman (a.k.a Wounded Healer) - they must undergo a ritual death. In Western psychological traditions this has been interpreted as a death for the ego and its personae; the letting go of a formerly constructed self-identity. In this world-view, wisdom is gained through initiation which breaks apart limited ideas of self so that larger ones can emerge. We become more fully ourselves through the process of initiation.

As I read, I began to understand that I had been experiencing my own psychological initiation. I could see that, before I could comprehend the complexities of such a process, I needed to complete it.. Only then could I begin to recognize the greater patterns and purpose behind my experiences and the habitual writing inclination they seeded inside me.

Initiatory rites of passage are generally divided into three stages. The first stage involves separation from the "known" world, the "known" identity. Initiation rituals often include brutal physical, psychological, and emotional tests of strength intended to break down any self-concept the initiate may have. After surviving challenging and perilous conditions, the initiate is often forced into seclusion in the wilderness and left alone to face the fears that inevitably arise from within.

The next stage is marked by complete loss of self. It involves the death of the previous self and a complete dismantling of the former way of life. It is a time of utter dissolution – the coming apart in order to come back together into a new form. This is the crux of transformation. The old dies. The new is born. In the third and final stage, the newly transformed individual returns to the world bearing treasures acquired on the journey.

The purpose of such rituals is to learn to transmute the prior, more limited self into a renewed, expanded being and to re-emerge, re-aggregate into culture wearing a new role and carrying new levels of responsibility. Such traditions date back thousands of years and can be found in all parts of the world. Initiation is an archetypal (universal) experience that eventually arises, in one form or another, in the life of every individual. The point is to usher each of us forward toward our own unique purpose in life and to equip us to face our destinies.

In my case, I needed to complete the cycle of coming apart and coming back together before I was able to see the patterns present in my initiatory journey and before I could begin to glimpse a larger purpose behind my obsessive writing habit. I had to come closer to understanding who I am, the shape of my own destiny, and a *raison d'etre* for the body of poems I'd been amassing for years.

Growing up, as I did, in the United States on the cusp of the Twentieth and Twenty First Centuries in a culture bereft of a deep-rooted, cohesive spiritual tradition, I didn't have initiatory guides (in the traditional sense) steering me through the periods of death and rebirth that lead to transformation. My personal rite of passage spanned decades and took on a form of its own. It has taken me years to begin understanding that my initiatory experiences have been contained and guided by my own soul and the world soul which have spoken to me, largely, through nature, art, and poetry.

Only now, after having undergone years upon years of physical, psychological, and emotional tests of strength; after having my character built only to be destroyed over and over again; after finally surrendering my personal will and ego over to a larger "intelligence" (the Jungian *Self*), have I finally begun to understand the many parallels running between the paths I have walked and the initiatory trials historically undertaken by the keepers of a culture's deeper, often hidden wisdom.

I could spend years and thousands of pages describing the challenges I have encountered and the lessons I have gleaned in turn. Perhaps one day I will do this, in a future book. For now, I chose to let the poetic voice speak, let the prose and poems tell for me the story of my passage and my re-emergence.

As I wrote the poems you are about to read, I had no intention of sharing them. Now, from my current vantage point, I see potential and perhaps a larger purpose for these poems beyond what I previously imagined. A wiser voice than my own gently reminds me that this work is not my own. It has moved through me and is meant to enter the world. It has been healing to me but it doesn't end there. From the bits of sharing I've done, I have been shown a greater gift. At times, some of these poems have been affirming and even healing for others (so I've been told). And that is what this work, this book is really about.

It's about restoring and mending that which is broken. It is about going to the edges to find the ancient medicine of repair and coaxing life out of decay. What does it mean to coax life out of decay, to breathe in the collapse and exhale renewed hope? It means taking the shit of life and using it to fertilize new growth. I have done this in my own life, in many ways, but largely through writing and image making. I have taken the pain and turned it into art. I have taken fear and generated strength from it. I have been sorting through chaos and looking for patterns, organizing and creating order wherever I can. I have used the challenge and adversity fated me to develop and refine my character in hopes of one day living more fully into my soul's purpose. This is what I've been up to for decades.

I have died and rebirthed myself many times by following my intuition and trusting in powers that lie beyond me, powers which I cannot begin to logically explain. I don't entirely know how I've done what I've done, only that I *have* done it. I also know that this process…I don't even know what to call it…the process of using shit constructively…is a lost art that is seeking revival. It's not even like I've heard the proverbial "call" and answered. I have embodied my art from the beginning. It isn't something I was taught, it is what my deepest self has guided me to do, to be. It comes to me naturally, which does not mean that it has been easy or that I have not been tasked with fully and consciously participating in the process. I have. It has come naturally and yet I have still had to step up and say "yes!" to my inner guidance system at every turn. And when I have failed to step up, there have been uncomfortable consequences, thus ensuring motivation to say yes, even when resistance is strong.

What I do know is that I have chosen to trust invisible forces beyond my comprehension. I have often chosen to follow vague intuitive hunches over logic. I have feared, I have doubted, I have questioned, I have wavered. And I am constantly relearning, sometimes with pain and difficulty, that I can and must trust my intuition and promptings from what I now think of as my soul, my spirit, and various divine interveners.

I have followed my inner guide into the darkness and have found treasures in its depths. I have many tales of these adventures and misadventures and perhaps part of my personal inheritance of the ancient medicines lies in recovering these tales, brushing them off and telling them. Perhaps. I have, after all, discovered that I, like my ancestors, am a story teller. This is part of my medicine. I'm still not exactly sure what it means to be a story teller, or what that looks like for me. This is all still a work in progress. But this book marks the beginning of my conscious emergence onto the storyteller path.

I do know that the hardships I have endured and the joys I have been blessed with (which have been encapsulated in these poems) have gifted me with precious bits of wisdom that carry an inevitable and unavoidable responsibility. My tale is a string of storylines shared among countless women, children, and men of the world. My voice is but one echo of thousands, perhaps millions of voices ringing out; a mirror reflection of the silent watch kept by those still recovering or discovering their own beautiful, unique voices.

In the hope that my private tribulations have not been entirely in vain, I share these writings publically with you, my valued reader. May they touch your heart, your mind, your soul, your spirit. May they inspire you to help secure a world where pain, frustration, repression and oppression no longer serve as a major fuel igniting the creative fires that burn within us all.

I pray, let my words penetrate the darker regions of the world-mind and illuminate them with the light of compassion, love, and truth. May they help kindle the highest and best revolutionary passions needed to make the changes necessary for the survival and evolution of our race and of all life on and in this magnificent planet. Blessed Be.

About the Artwork

The Illustrations on the front cover and at the beginning of each section are reproductions of collages I began creating in 2000. They are an experiment in creative play that I took up one evening after reading about the Exquisite Corpse or *cadavre exquis* game created by the French Surrealists. It started as a word game in which one person would write a line and then cover it and pass it to the next person who would add onto it, not knowing what the person before had written. In the end, weird and wonderful compositions would emerge.

It soon developed into a drawing game, along the same lines, in which each participant added to an image only partially revealed. The resulting composite image was fantastic and absurd. I decided to cut up a book of old, no longer copyrighted graphic art and place the images together into unexpected combinations, à la the Surrealists. I found some of the configurations to be rather unsettling and unappealing, but a few intrigued me. Upon closer examination, they appeared to be a peculiar sort of map, or perhaps a narrative, of certain regions or aspects of psyche – both personal and collective. Making my own Exquisite Corpses became an amusing and curious pastime.

When I was assembling this book, it became clear that certain of these collages were uncannily befitting the various sections of poetry. The very idea of an exquisite corpse is an intentional paradox, and paradox is a seminal inspiration for my work. I couldn't have planned it better if I tried. I'm grateful to the original illustrators who penned each image and to the Surrealists for the inspiration. *Merci à ceux qui sont venus avant moi et m'a inspire.*

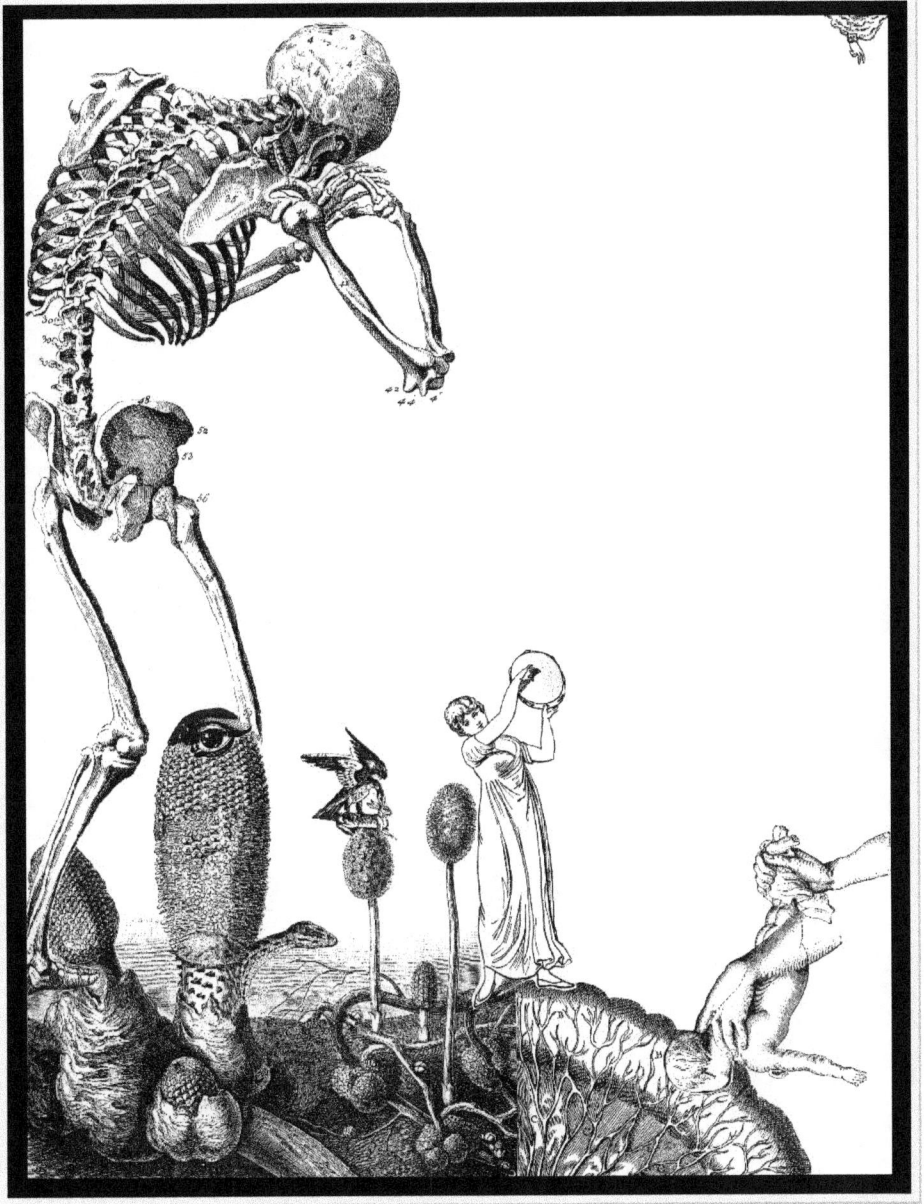

PART ONE

13

We all have stories: individual stories; familial stories; cultural stories; and an emerging global story that is at once incredible and terrifying. Sometimes our tales entwine and weave together harmoniously. But not always. Sometimes our stories collide, ripping and tearing the delicate tapestry of life. I believe there is great value in excavating and sharing our often painful stories of yesterday. I believe we must, at the same time, pay close attention to the stories we create for tomorrow. If we are to address our personal and collective disrepair we must have the courage to look into the dark and shadowy places within ourselves and our societies. We live in the world our ancestors dreamed up and our descendants will inherit the world of our dreams. What stories were we handed? What stories will we pass on?

My ancestors were storytellers. I am a storyteller. Before I share legends of my people; before I tell tales that come to me from across vast and distant lands; before I sweep up specks of ancient story dust and shape them into soft and moldable mythic clay; I must first tell you my story. My story is a continuation of my ancestors' stories. My tale is part of a global narrative. Many women and men share threads of my story. In some ways, my story may be your story. On different days the threads of my story-web take on different colors of the rainbow, each a carefully spun filament capturing a different ray of light. The thread that connects all of the strands in my story-web is a delicate string of transformation. This is the weaving together of my yesterday threads with the fibers of my tomorrow. Here, past meets present in order to change the future.

A speck of story dust

I was born in the dead of winter. Where I come from, it's the season when the natural world sleeps under blankets of snow. Plants die back to the earth and trees send all of their life force back down into their roots. Insects die or lie dormant and animals retreat to hibernate in dens and caves. In the frozen death time, my life began.

It was late morning when I entered the world. Late morning is my time of day, the time of day when I wake up and come to life, the time of day when I am finally ready to let the world in. Before then I am in womb time. I need my solitude. Those who know me well save the big questions and conversations until after noon.

I was born in Denver Colorado, the "mile high city," where the air is thin at 5,280 feet above sea level. I lived there until my 33rd year. It is a strange city, sprouting up on a barren landscape. The high desert -

harsh, dry, hot, cold. Extreme. Not much grows there. Not much thrives. That which does survive the intense climate must be able to endure extremes – extremes in temperature, in weather patterns, and in topography. Droughts are common as are flash floods. The summer sun will scald the skin off your nose as will the winter wind. Rugged mountains jut out abruptly from quietly undulating plains. Icy rivers plunge down steep canyons with urgent and deadly speed to pool silently in placid, mirrored lakes and ponds. Steel and concrete dominate the cityscape and industry stains the sky and earth along the front range of the Rockies.

Not much is gentle or gradual in the high desert except the sunrise and the sunset. These were always my favorite times, times of transition. Some say that at twilight the boundaries between worlds shift and open. As a child watching the golden orange Colorado sunsets I could stretch my mind across a threshold and imagine the men and women who once populated the region. I could see the unspoiled plains with the majestic Rocky Mountains cutting up through them. I could see the world as it was in ancient times. This was not a settling place. This was a land of transition. This was the land of the nomads, the land of the buffalo. Villages were not built here. People did not come to stay.

I believe that the land has a hand in shaping the people who inhabit it, even in modern times. I find the people born and raised in Colorado tend to be like the high desert - sharp, rough, rugged, restless, and intensely beautiful. Survivors. Perhaps I will forever have a love-hate relationship with the land of my birth. It gave me life and brought me continual death.

Mine was not a happy childhood. Maybe happy is the wrong word. I was a surprisingly happy child but my childhood was not light, was not easy. It was prickly like the cactus garden I fell into at age five. I was covered from head to toe with cactus needles that my mother meticulously tried to pick out one by one. Try as she may, she just couldn't get them all. She told me that in time they would fester and my body would push them to the surface in a river of pus. I find that to be true in life. We get poked, jabbed, penetrated by outside forces. If we don't pluck away the remaining debris it will sit below the surface, quietly festering, to one day pop out onto the exterior as a big ugly boil that we simply can't ignore. My life is full of big ugly boils.

The Point

You learned to survive
As a shape shifter
The cement that held the post in place
As the other children climbed
Up and down
Back and forth
This side, that side
Of the fence
You knew the center
The pivotal point
From which all other points radiate
It is where you started
And where you always returned
Like a spider
At the center of her web
Weaving out an alphabet
Of distress signals
Tapping them out on the telephone poles
With your woodpecker beak
But your point was always lost
In the translation
Always interrupted by the ringing phone
And all the grown-ups
Who never seemed to have any point
So you made yourself a weather vane
Spinning in the wind
From the rooftop you could see
The lay of the land
And watch the sun set in fire
Over the mountains
As you rounded your sharp points
Into a smooth circle of digits
You would dance around
From the point
At the center of the circumference
Your second hand
Always ticking away the moments
Before the moon rose crescent silver
And you would wrap it around your neck

Like the last great woman-pharaoh
Empress of the ancient pyramids
Projecting up from four corners
Pointing at constellations
In the distant black
Wide-open pupils
Pulling it downward
To the point within
The darkness that pushed itself upon you
Drawing you out into a thin line
Then snapping you back to a single point
A polka-dot spot on a bed sheet
A speck of dirt on the bottom of a shoe
A drop of ink on a blank page
A period at the end of a sentence

The shadowed aspects of my childhood were dark and oppressive, painfully squeezing my molecules into sharp, penetrating focus. Like a diamond blade able to cut through the hardest material, I had the ability to penetrate density and darkness with x-ray vision. Perhaps I was born with the ability to perceive things with laser focus. Or perhaps it was a skill I acquired in the dark and silent hours of the night while I laid awake, alert, prepared. Two of my gifts - I am alert and aware. Not much slips past my penetrating gaze. I live in a heightened state of awareness. Sometimes it is helpful, sometimes it is exhausting. One of several proverbial blessings and simultaneous curse ensembles I was bestowed with.

On the shadowy end of the spectrum, I was a young witness to the over-consumption of alcohol, the cold and clammy hand of despair, depression, repression, the iron fist of bottled rage. I am a survivor of childhood sexual abuse, among other things. I took my environment in on deep and complex levels. Try as I may to shut out a world of sadness and sickness, I took it all in. I saw, I heard, I felt. I locked it away in the catacombs of forgotten memories.

I recorded it and tucked it all away like Thoth, the ancient Egyptian scribe, the record keeper. Or perhaps I was more like his lesser known female counter-part, Seshat, the Egyptian goddess of history and books whose name means "she who scrivens." Inventor of writing, keeper of records, knowledge and wisdom, Seshat secretly presided over my inner hall of records, recording my passage and storing it away for future reflection.

From eternity, she beckons. "Look into the mirror of time..."

My childhood was intense and confusing. It has marked my life. In many ways, it has determined my path as a healer and artist. So much pain and darkness threatened to tear me apart at the core. I spent my days seeking escape and relief. As a child, I found it in the imaginal world of fantasy, fairy tales, film, the arts, and in nature. I sought solace in the pictures I created, in the magical stories my aunts, uncles, and grandparents told me, and in the books my mother read aloud. This contact with the mythic realm pulled me out of the darkness of abuse and grounded me firmly into a reality that I could grasp, a world that I could live and function within. Thankfully, even in childhood I had tools that helped me stay connected to the light within my own soul. Despite the positive things that offset the trauma, fragmentation still occurred and integration was interrupted in my psyche. The split occurred and my world was divided into stark polarities. My life was shaped and formed by exaggerated dualities that colored every aspect of my waking world.

Torn

Torn like a thorn ripping through the tender flesh
Confused in two worlds that by nature do not mesh
Divided like a canyon that separates the land
Undecided like the dice held within the dealer's hand
Wanting to be kind with a soul that's filled with rage
Not knowing what I'll find every time I turn the page
Trying to be gentle in a world that's full of hate
Feeling rather mental in this contradictive state
Sometimes I want to heal it upon the sacred mound
Or maybe just conceal it as I crush it to the ground
But I am driven onward by a strong need to create
Yet sometimes it's hard to focus in this life obscured by fate
An easier existence I long for in my dreams
But the path of least resistance isn't always what it seems
So I live with the torment of this life misunderstood
Always opening up doorways that I never knew I could

But nothing leads me closer to the answers that I seek
Nothing external to define if I am strong or I am weak
No one to truly grasp all these dilemmas in my brain
Just those who stand outside and judge if I'm a genius or insane

I have had a lifelong struggle with an innate need to express and communicate the very things I don't want anyone to know about, the things I desperately don't want to share. It has been a painfully inconvenient push-and-pull dynamic within my psyche. It is confusing to experience things that others believe are impossible. It's not easy knowing things that others try to hide - from you, from the world, and even from themselves. I was inwardly compelled to communicate what I perceived and experienced while outwardly petrified to do so. It is not fun to be the messenger when the message is one that causes a backlash of pain, revulsion and fear. What do you do with a gift like this?

I went through various stages of expression and repression. I would choose silence until I could no longer bear the weight of it. I would speak my truth and as those around me recoiled into strike poses like the rattlesnakes I was cautioned to avoid, I would bite my own forked tongue and apologize for an uncontrolled outbreak of honesty. Oops. This is no way to live a life. There were so many assertions, direct and indirect, telling me to keep my mouth shut, to tune out, to turn away, to dull my mind. So many that I started repressing my thoughts and then creatively regurgitating poetry and art about the dark and shadowy world I was all too aware of.

I'll give you a lollipop if you don't tell. I'll make you wish you were never born if you do tell.

Do tell. Do tell.

History/Herstory

He is not the root, only the stem.
He holds the history of those before him,
the pain, the suffering, he too is a channel.

My roots connect to her,
the punished, the sufferer,
exiled into silence.
I hear her voice calling through the centuries,
building strength,
wounded but not defeated,
strong and wise.
There is beauty in her pain
and with pain comes the great lesson of healing.

c.1998

Matriarchal Prayer

I carry your pain inside me
like the pit at the core
of the sweetest fruit
The seeds
of your fears and dreams
have blossomed inside
I breathe my life into them
and make them my own
In me they grow
and surface for the world
to look upon
with affection or disgust
My soul stripped down
Bare to the world
I am the crystallization
and magnification
of all you have ever been
I am the one
to face the demons
You have eluded for so long
I have all of your strengths
and my own
I stand in confrontation
My bow stretched tight
My aim piercing and true
An arrow to the heart
I would could I walk back in time
And heal all your wounds
but I can now only heal my own
Someday these injuries
we have suffered
will be but scars
Speaking stories of a past
our great-granddaughters
will tell their granddaughters
as if they were myths
and not the truths
We have lived through
and struggled against

for ages
It stirs inside my soul
I bring it out into the light
so there is darkness no more
I pray peace
for those before me
and those yet unborn
May our blood purify within me
and be forever changed
through my beating heart

c.1999

Afterthoughts

Do you know I still remember
You hoped I would forget
My words now will remind you
And fill you with regret
Did it make you feel so powerful
The weak conquered by the strong
You forgot about my feelings
You ignored that you were wrong
I'm here to bring it up again
To shout it to the world
Go on and tell just how it felt
To control a little girl
I was no more than a child
Confused and very scared
I have grown into a woman
I hope you are prepared
To face the consequences
Of the damage you have done
I am in control now
My story has just begun
Someday I'll sing it loudly
So that everyone can hear
How you raped my body
And filled my soul with fear
Guess you should have figured
One day my heart would heal
My sadness turn to anger
And the truth I would reveal
I hope that you can face it
Someday you'll have no choice
You will sink in silence
While I shall find my voice

c.1993

I See Her

I see her now.
She is but a child,
no more than eight or nine.
Her sky blue dress pressed
against her body by the force
of the wind. I see her
long golden braids tied up
with satin bows. She looks
to the sky in wonder.
Her mind drifts
in and out of a world filled
with magic and dreams.
I see her bend
to the earth she gathers
dandelions scattered
about her feet. She choses
each one with care,
aware of the life
contained within each petal.
She sits on the soft
summer grass, weaving
flowers in a ring
while thinking upon
the ones she dearly loves.
She feels the fleeting flicker
of this life and knows this
moment is fleeing.
She sees to the time when
those she knows will
be gone.
She knows that one day she will be
gone too.
She lays back and closes
her eyes. She feels
the wind sweeping across her body.
She takes comfort in the beauty
that surrounds her.
There is wisdom in her innocence
and power in her pain.   c. 1996

Wonder

Don't you wonder why
Some eyes open while others close
Don't you wonder why
A seed never planted never grows
Don't you wonder why
A man can walk but cannot fly
Don't you wonder why
The eyes can never tell a lie
Don't you wonder why
The human world is one of strife
Don't you wonder why
The wells of water spring up life
Don't you wonder why
They say that dreams keep you alive
Don't you wonder why
It seems by quest you won't arrive
Don't you wonder why
It seems the question is the key
Don't you wonder why
It seems the answer sets you free

c.1988

The Scar

The scar is there,
thick and wide.
Why don't I remember
when the truth lies
stretched beneath
fearful fingertips?
I close my eyes.
My breathing becomes
shallow. Solar plexus collapse
inward, like a black hole
extinguishing all light.
A tremor starts
at the top of my head
and travel down
the length of my body.
What could it be?
My memory drifts to hazy,
tear stained visions of black
and red and cheap
velvet portraits. My heart
dances in my chest
in rhythmic horror.
A scream builds
in the bowels of my belly, pushing
upward with the force of a hurricane
at its heels. Nothing
comes. It is swallowed
so as not to be released.
A gray melancholia swells
behind my eyes and fastens a knot
at the back of my throat.
Why can't I remember?
The scar remains,
like a footprint frozen
in time, petrified by silence.
It marks me like a symbol.
Of what?.... I'm not sure.
The story is lost,
until I find it again.
c. 1992

The Point

You learned to survive
As a shape shifter
The cement that held the post in place
As the other children climbed
Up and down
Back and forth
This side, that side
Of the fence
You knew the center
The pivotal point
From which all other points radiate
It is where you started
And where you always returned
Like a spider
At the center of her web
Weaving out an alphabet
Of distress signals
Tapping them out on the telephone poles
With your woodpecker beak
But your point was always lost
In the translation
Always interrupted by the ringing phone
And all the grown-ups
Who never seemed to have any point
So you made yourself a weather vane
Spinning in the wind
From the rooftop you could see
The lay of the land
And watch the sun set in fire
Over the mountains
As you rounded your sharp points
Into a smooth circle of digits
You would dance around
From the point
At the center of the circumference
Your second hand
Always ticking away the moments
Before the moon rose crescent silver
And you would wrap it around your neck

Like the last great woman-pharaoh
Empress of the ancient pyramids
Projecting up from four corners
Pointing at constellations
In the distant black
Wide-open pupils
Pulling it downward
To the point within
The darkness that pushed itself upon you
Drawing you out into a thin line
Then snapping you back to a single point
A polk-a-dot spot on a bed sheet
A speck of dirt on the bottom of a shoe
A drop of ink on a blank page
A period at the end of a sentence

c. 2002

Torn

Torn like a thorn ripping through the tender flesh
Confused in two worlds that by nature do not mesh
Divided like a canyon that separates the land
Undecided like the dice held within the dealer's hand
Wanting to be kind with a soul that's filled with rage
Not knowing what I'll find every time I turn the page
Trying to be gentle in a world that's full of hate
Feeling rather mental in this contradictive state
Sometimes I want to heal it upon the sacred mound
Or maybe just conceal it as I crush it to the ground
But I am driven onward by my desire to create
Yet sometimes it's hard to focus in this life obscured by fate
An easier existence I long for in my dreams
But the path of least resistance isn't always what it seems
So I live with the torment of this life misunderstood
Always opening up doorways that I never knew I could
But nothing leads me closer to the answers that I seek
Nothing external to define if I am strong or I am weak
No one to truly grasp all these dilemmas in my brain
Just those who stand outside and judge if I'm a genius or insane

c. 1990

Have/Not

To have
    To have not
Helped to grow
    Forced to rot
Forms different lives
    Breeds different thoughts
Who is buying
    Who is bought?
Obscuring truth
    Dividing man
The ones who can't
    The ones who can
The trampled foot
    The ruling hand
The stepping stone
    The master plan

c.1990

Think About It All

I watch the rust and amber leaves fall silently on displaced earth,
and I think   about it all.
I hear crows caw wizened warnings to a world too rushed to care,
and I think   about it all.
I see forests cleared as traffic flashes by in tactless discontent,
and I think   about it all.
I watch the sunken faces of strangers with deep and hollowed eyes,
and I think   about it all.
I feel the sun's silent rays penetrate my skin and bake Earth's crust,
and I think   about it all.
I fill my lungs with crisp autumn air, take in the pungent progress,
and I think   about it all.

c. 1994

Alone

She sits alone
Removed from the tyranny
  of their day to day to day
She shouts out
But no one seems to hear
So she sits alone and watches
Reflections of the ages
  course through her veins
No one notices
   that the earth shivers
    beneath their sleeping feet
No one cares
  that the walls are cracking
    and weeping around them
They fail to observe
  the rhythms of the moon
They don't understand
  that they cannot hold
    what they cannot grasp
Like ghosts they fade
  into the dingy tapestries draping
    the halls of the haunted city
So she sits alone and watches
She spies their back alley daydreams
  pouring from glasses
    into the gutters
Their sideways love
  slipping through crevices
    running into the streets
They are not like her
They do not seek answers
  They don't see the tides swell and break
    or consider the cycles of seedlings
They don't understand
  that they cannot control
    what they cannot comprehend
So she sits alone and watches

c. 1991

On My Own

Please open up your eyes
and take a look around
You think it's building up
but it's really falling down
I try to help you see
but you don't seem to care
It's clear my good intentions
will not get me anywhere
As long as I stay here
my vision will be clouded
When I look for open space
I see that it's already crowded
When I seek around for refuge
I find nothing there to hide me
The only home I've ever known
is residing deep inside me
Seems I'm alone in trying
to set the record straight
And help will not arrive
no matter how long I wait
I'm searching high and low
for a sign out there to show me
which way I need to go
to find someone who'll know me
If I release my fears
I might move out of this phase
Discover clues inside me
to guide me out of this maze
In my heart I've always known
that I truly am alone
And if I'm gonna make it
I have to do it on my own

c. 1989

When Will I Learn

How many times will I walk upon fire
    before I will finally wear shoes
How many fences must I leap over
    Before I will open the gate
How many times must I stumble through darkness
    Before I will turn on the light
How long must I swim in an ocean of sorrow
    Before I will rest on the shore

c. 1987

Modern Myth

humans are made from corn
except for white men, they say
they come from ants

always busy cleaning, clearing
gathering, sorting, labeling
hurry, hurry,
this way, that way
grab it all up and
hurry back
to the congested metro-hill-habitat
running, running,
climbing over one another to
get there
faster, faster,
this way, that way

busy, busy collective mind of
greed and power
produces a corrupted colony of
confusion and chaos
working busily under the
illusion of progress
hurry, hurry
explore, exploit
gather it up and
hurry back
busy, busy,
consuming the resources
of Mother Earth

forgetting the spirit of the corn
forgetting the spirit of the earth

c. 1993

No Feeling

Sometimes I wish I didn't feel anything at all
My own life seems so removed
when I see your face proud and strong
as your fields are burned and your children wait for death
It tears at my soul
I see Him encircle you like a vulture
pecking slowly away at all that is sacred and pure
thrusting his vile lust through the core of your spirit
as He has done for centuries
like you're some cheap whore
Sometimes I wonder how He doesn't feel anything at all

c. 2001

White Father

It is I
my white father
who through the chaos
and confusion
of my uprooted existence
have drank from the well
of ancient understanding
in the world of the wise
and bring it to your eyes
to your ears
through a long trail
of conquest
and the irony
of coincidence
It is I
my white father
who translates the tongues
of the sages you slaughter
for you who can hear
only the words of
your forefathers
the sound of
your own voice and
the voices in your head
that ring louder than
the screams
of ten thousand babies
that die by your
sacrificial sword
It is I
my white father
who strains
under the shackles
of your doctrine and dogma
which have chained me
to your impoverished soul
and left me searching
the teachings
of the savages

you destroy in fear
my skin reflects
the color of your hatred
but my soul screams
with savage fury
being born of your blood
of your lustful spirit
It is I
my white father
who finds more truth
in the rivers and trees
than in your
systems and structures
it is I
who watches your ways
and traces your tracks
with medicine to mend
what you infect
as you pass in haste
and erase in ignorance
It is I
my white father
who finds you
to be the most savage
one of us all

c. 1997

Through Chaos

What cannot
be fixed
must be
destroyed and
created anew
not recreated in the
same image
created anew
Maybe it's okay
to be
in chaos
Maybe by being
in chaos
we become aware
of rhythms and pulses
ways of maneuvering
through chaos
and finding
new truths
new thoughts
new words
creating new worlds
the effect
of which
cannot be known
or it wouldn't
be new
Maybe it's okay to
not know
Maybe it's better to
realize
we've never really
known
to begin with

c. 1999

Profound Nature

My story
is not a tragedy
it is a
triumph
of the most profound
nature
it can't be seen
from the
outside
for it dwells
within
love has conquered
pain and fear
through it all
I keep my heart
I will not grow
bitter
I am filled with
love
no matter the depth of
suffering
I am woman
I am strong
I still love
feelings
experiences
come and go
but love resides
within my heart
for eternity
nothing in
this world
can rob me of that
for me this is
triumph
success
of the most profound
nature
c. 1998

PART TWO

I was born in Mercy hospital.

Mercy me. Lord, have mercy on this child.

I was to be hospitalized in that same beautifully crafted historic building fourteen years later as a teenaged drug abuser and "mental health" patient. A child of mercy in the hands of a merciless system - misunderstood, feared, and locked up "for my own safety".

Ironically, separating me from my world actually served as my first real introduction to community, outside of family. I had always had groups of friends, but living with other juvenile misfits day in, day out, sharing our issues, which were too taboo to talk about in the outside world, was a whole new level of bonding. We spent our days and nights locked inside the sterile and structured, artificially aired and fluorescently lit compartments. Packed into our sixth floor pale green institutional wing, we had meetings and classes and chained smoked on breaks. It was the late 1980s and we smoked right there in the hospital, at the end of the two hallways that made up our intimate little wing. There were big glass windows that let in light and a view of the city beyond. But they did not open to let in fresh air. It was a smoke chamber every few hours, like clockwork. Break time. Everybody smoke. A lot. I learned to blow smoke rings at the end of that hall, on a blue vinyl chair, looking out the windows at the tall and puffy Colorado cloud walls in the bright blue sky. Though I was the youngest kid in there, I felt like a wise caterpillar on a great mushroom.

Whoooo are yoouuu?
Who are yooooouuuuuu?

I already carried a fair share of Trickster energy, which stepped in and turned the hospitalization on its head. My life had grown quite topsy-turvy, so I befriended that energy and used it to my advantage. I played a very convincing Pollyanna and had the staff swayed into believing I was not so far progressed down the path of trouble-courtin', trouble-findin', trouble-makin'.

I was minding my own business, trying to attend to my tiresome lessons when along came a white rabbit.

If they had had a crystal ball, they would've seen that I was lying. They could've perhaps more accurately predicted the fate of my future.

But as it was, they could not see beyond the curtain, and I, well, I was worthy of an Oscar. I smiled softly as I brushed away the crocodile tears from my Nile blue eyes and I was released ahead of schedule.

Three years later I was hospitalized again. It was late winter, February 29, 1988. Leap day. The invisible day that only shows itself every four years. I had just turned seventeen. The gray sky was thick as mud hanging like dripping, dirty laundry over my head. The Rocky Mountains create an air trap over the city of Denver. *Stagnation. Density.* The pristine snow was pierced by the blackened molecules of exhaust. *Exhaust.* The sun always shines, no matter how bitter cold the air. Its appearance is deceptive. The trees are naked and touched by the fondling fingers of frost. To survive in the winter everything living must go underground.

Underground. The only life is underground. Down, down in the dungeons. Awake. Alive. Awake. Alive underground.

This time, I had gone so far down the rabbit hole, I couldn't talk my way back up to the surface. And I didn't have the energy or interest, this time, in making up salvation stories. My reality was already a haphazardly spun yarn. Rather than endlessly spinning away, I let myself free fall into the underworld. Like Persephone abducted, I was staining my lips with pomegranate seeds while welcoming the souls of the recently deceased. Everything was on hold in the upper world, the outer world of my just-turned-seventeen life. All of my energy withdrew into the deathlike dreamtime. I was afloat on the river Styx, my little vessel oared by the ghostly apparitions, thorazine and lithium. Oh, my wraithlike brothers, constant companions through the antiseptic halls of my confinement. Bearing out our sentences, hand in hand, side by side.

...and they drew all manner of things – everything that begins with an M – such as mousetraps, and the moon, and memory, and much-ness... (Lewis Carroll)

I was locked up from the outside, but more importantly (and painfully) I was locked up on the inside. This time, my Trickster stirred the pot with sticky truths I tried not to hide. Hiding gets so tiresome.

Your rules do not apply to me, don't you see. I step beyond the boundaries of your influence with ease. I may look like you, but I am not of your world. Honey-haired, I scamp through the halls of under-land, where you dare not tramp for fear of getting lost.

    The more I rebelled, the harder they clamped down on me. The lock-down took many different forms, but the gist of it was about making me smaller, duller, and quieter than I truly am.

I have hidden
a spool of thread in my pocket
Locked it away from view
you didn't notice it
on the way in

late at night
as the guards change posts
and ghosts enter my room
before I drown in a
lithium pool
I escape through the roof
weave a ladder to the moon

Loose threads gather there
stairway to celestial rings
string tied around my finger
I shall not forget

Frequently summoned
I spend the darker hours
in the tower of the sun
Under showers of grace
that erase what ails me

I return before first light
With a mended heart and
moon dust encrusted fingernails
an incurable star twinkle
winking in my eyes
which annoys you to no end

I was transforming my dreams into comprehensive blueprints I stashed away for my future self. She'll know where to find them.

Follow the thread.

In due time, after much probing and prodding and poking, I was released in accord with the insurance company's schedule. There are limits to the cost of reform. I was set free as a surprisingly changed self into an indefinably changed reality, both of which I no longer recognized.

I was not the girl I was before, or before, or before that. I had already been stripped of the accoutrements of my identity so many times, like the ancient Sumerian Queen Inanna on her descent. My ego was challenged, bared, and humbled at each gate of my adolescent initiation. I descended. And then I returned, mysteriously renewed by the painful process of dismemberment. Released back into the upper world, I walked undisguised under the freshly re-starred nights of my freedom.

Hello world! I have returned, flower sprung from the mysteries of the fertile decay, opening to the rays of moon and daylight at last. At last!

I never finished high school. I was done with four-walled institutions, of education, or otherwise. I was restless and ready to live a life bursting at the seams. The typical American teen life did not interest me. I was unreasonably dynamic, fast-changing, too easily bored, and quickly disinterested. I outgrew things the moment I grew into them. As soon as I arrived, I was ready to move on. Never settling, I was attuned to the rhythm of the plains. My inner nomad always watching the horizon line for that which was coming toward me or passing out of sight.

I had already come to realize that I had completely different ideas (from the ones I'd been spoon fed) on performance and achievement. After the second hospitalization, I refused reintegration into the artificially sweetened world of public high school. Too sticky and cloying. I was like an irritable transplant organ that would not adapt itself to the host body it was being forced into. It was not a good fit. *Uh-uh, this is not my home.*

At the time I didn't give a fuck about a future I couldn't connect with. I couldn't bring myself to care about what my peers or the adults around me wanted or expected of me. I wasn't *playing* the part of a rebel.

I was *living* my inner Trickster. I was running cheek to cheek with my own instincts and impulses, allowing deeper internal stirrings to compel and propel me forward with wicked speed.

I couldn't manage to mold myself to anybody's idea of who I *should* be. I wasn't trying to be "somebody", and I had outgrown trying to "fit in." I was who I was. My ego had already been torn apart by the trauma wolves. I was already so picked apart by the vultures that I was in the process of being digested and expelled as a fertile little pellet. Magnetic at my core, I pointed to my own true North. My inner compass became the only thing I could rely on (even when it led me astray.) There was something wildly liberating about my ability to self-orient and navigate. And though I didn't realize it at the time, there was also something terribly isolating about my staunch emotional and psychological self-sufficiency. I was a survivor who was quick with my sword. Cutting and clearing became a way of life.

My young and precocious eyes turned away from text books toward "real life," and I was drawn to culture's gritty, smelly underbelly. I needed to satiate my gnawing hunger for real adventure. I needed to Experience The World. High school dances, clubs, activities, athletics, homework, college prep.... what? By the time I was sixteen, that world was more foreign and distant to me than Easter Island. The stadium lights blinded and disturbed me. My curiosity led me away from the well-lit avenue parades and pom-poms. While the marching band skillfully played, I dipped around the corner into the twisting dark passageways. I slipped into the dimly lit back alleys to find my education waiting for me with a shiny ticket and dark glint in his eyes.

Turning

Eyes swollen like rushing rivers
Trying to hold back a flood
Pain buried deep in the landscape
The face of the earth stained with blood
Penetrating darkness invading
Soul ravaged raped and cut deep
The enemy crawls through the shadows
Raging winds tormenting sleep
Storm clouds thick and condensing
Prefer to obscure than to weep
Silence the rage with the fear grip
Promise lies that forever can't keep
Truths buried like treasures in mountains
Or like walking a land filled with mines
No matter the care of the passer
Detonation's a matter of time

c. 1995

The Fall

Speeding 'round curves, death pasted to grills
    Like fears in a basement stairway
Where all that I love becomes all that I hate
    And illusions begin to engulf me
I light candles in daytime and sink down deeply
    In a void that seems to surround me
I listen to messages inside my head
    And follow the way that they point me
I open the doors to randomized chance
    In hope that my future will find me
As daylight dissolves and darkness descends
    It leaves no lights to guide me
Dancing in circles, down side city streets
    I seek all from which I've been hiding
I lower my head in a silent entreaty
    That someday the truth will unbind me
I look to the sky and read signs that instruct
    To avoid anything angry
I close my eyes and wonder how I can ever
    Avoid what dwells deep inside me

c. 1996

No More

In a box
Chains and locks
Student listens
Teacher talks
Shoes in the hall
Lies on the wall
The longer I listen
The deeper I fall
Into numb apathy
Not where I want to be
Drawn to the street outside
This shit isn't for me
In a cage
With silent rage
They say it is
A passing stage
An issue that will pass
So keep me in the class
Infiltrate my brain
With concepts they contain
Stagnant and controlling
It's driving me insane
Born a rebel to the core
Their world it is a
ghastly bore
my truthful words
they can't ignore
I'll cross the floor
And find the door
No need to fear
I'm out of here
Can't sit here anymore

c. 1987

Time Bomb

Inner city sun set
Blood red black sky
Raven kids
Pills, thrills, spills
On the unforgiving
slab, jab, grab
All you can before it's gone
The wind bites cold on
the Polyester landfill
skirt, flirt, hurt
Be careful what you say
Semi-permanent latex tower
always hears all
call, fall, crawl
Into the sweetly
seeping underground
Rip the foundation down
to rhythms of the
stars, scars, bars
Wipe it all out
Like a blistering time bomb
On the face of eternity
Caught in a groove
It's time to move
Into the next dimension
Are you coming?

c. 1988

A Little Lost

I was drenched in the stench
    with the walls closing in
the air thick and heavy
    my head began to spin
the night was dark around me
    I wandered through the maze
filled with indecision
    my mind lost in a daze
can't remember how I got here
    upon this twisted road
my heart downcast in anguish
    from my heavy load
staying in the shadows
    staring at the stars
I recognized the face of death
    and felt the sword of Mars

c. 1988

Live Wire

She is cold
Her hands are frozen
Her heart is numb
plastic wrap
and Styrofoam cups
cigarettes on an empty stomach
She feels nauseous
disconnected
from the telephone wires
from the gasoline fumes
parking lots and shopping mall discos
droning rhythms
through closed steel doors
steel knives stabbing gentle hopes
tears like molten steel
on stone cold features
visions of chaos
reflections from the moon
She hears his voice
and follows him into the dungeon
rabid hounds salivate
thirsty for young blood
eyes riveting through her body
She knows where the door is
She does not fear the frost
She does not know who she is
but she knows who she is not
the icy streets free her
She has no more blood to shed

c. 1989

Here

Here in this place
    I hear the sounds
        Of wish coins tossed in a well
Here in this place
    I see in your eyes
        Many stories you're waiting to tell
Seems I've sat here so long
    with the world rushing by
        I see it blur passed
    and I ask myself why
What brought me back
    and what makes me stay
Here in this place
    where I can't get away
        from the knife in my heart
        and the lies on your tongue
Not sure where to start
    As it all comes undone
So I feel like a ghost
    Not seen by the eye
        Not really alive
        yet unwilling to die
Here in this place
    Where my hopes and dreams fade
        and I feel like a shadow lost in the shade
            stuck in the game 'til the pieces are played
                Accepting decisions unaware I had made

c. 1995

Caged

When nothing holds meaning
and everything slips away
it washes into blackness
and falls into decay
convince yourself you're happy
in a darkened prison cell
create a pseudo heaven
within the depths of hell
look out through barred windows
watch the world go by
see it burn to ashes
in the blinking of an eye
think about your future
the day you will be free
prepare for your escape now
carve your name deeply
upon the stones that hold you
inside against your will
your body may enslave you
but your soul cannot be killed
someday you'll break beyond it
step out to open skies
inhale winds of freedom
live outside the lies
find the life your meant for
rise above your fate
understand your destiny
and love what you create

c. 1988

Reluctant Messenger

If I understood the reasons
It may help to ease the pain
of constant disappointment
a sky always filled with rain
It makes the land grow richer
the crops plentiful and strong
but weighs heavy on the psyche
to have no sunshine for so long
A few must make the payment
to bring awareness to the rest
The gift of inspiration
can be a knife into the chest
To aspire to the summit
is to sacrifice this life
to the hand of guiding wisdom
and the path obscured by strife
The lessons of the sages
comes with a heavy cost
With each turning of the pages
more ignorance is lost
Yet increasing knowledge
brings out into the light
aspects of reality
long hidden from my sight
To see through false impressions
to the truths that lie within
I see the blade that has two edges
The beginning and the end
And I learn the hardest lessons
Where there's yang there's always yin
that the demon of destruction
is creation's polar twin
There's no way to escape it
From life always follows death
And my words may not be noticed
until I breathe my final breath
I try hard to accept it
This ironic twist of fate
which tangles my desires

mixing love with hate
The hardest part is knowing
that all I have to say
isn't recognized as wisdom
doesn't change things either way

c.1997

Hidden Heart

To let go of control
and let the guard down
isn't easy for one
always playing the clown
who would rather a martyr
than a victim be found
who continues to cling
to an old thorny crown
to open one's heart
and be open to pain
to settle for loss
and not risk it for gain
to push away love
and turn away fame
to run from contentment
and in sorrow remain
is the way of a fool
whose heart has been broken
who swallows back words
that have never been spoken
fearing the ones
who can blast the heart open
but the look in their eyes
is a promising token
that one day they'll tear
the wall down to reveal
the depth of the soul
that they try to conceal
and all the emotions
they pretend not to feel
and a love that they hide
that is honest and real

c. 1990

Gypsy Soul

I have a gypsy spirit
I can't seem to control
and these wounds in my heart
sometimes I can't console
It's hard to trust people
in this wicked world
where I'm treated like no more
than a stupid helpless girl
I can't believe the things
that people say
they say what they want
just to get their way
they say that they care
when they really don't
and they say they'll be there
but I know that they won't
so I keep my heart hidden
underneath my sleeve
because before they arrive
they decide to leave
so I focus on myself
'cuz no one else is there
unconfined by my mind
I go everywhere
I will roam this earth
until I get bored
and I'll shout really loud
so I can't be ignored
and I'll forgive all of you
who have mistreated me
as I live out this bitter
sweet tragedy

c. 1989

Oh, woe
> The tables I've turned
>> The bridges I've burned
>>> The lessons I've learned

Oh, woe
> The games I have played
>> The friends I've betrayed
>>> The mistakes I have made

Oh, woe
> The times I have lied
>> The fears that I hide
>>> The truths I've denied

Oh, woe
> The truths I assert
>> The words that I blurt
>>> The people I've hurt

Oh, woe
> The ones that I blame
>> The parts that feel shame
>>> The sides I can't tame

Oh, woe
> The pain I have felt
>> The past places I've dwelt
>>> The cards I've been dealt

c.1989

Same Pain

Here I sit
By the water
Just like years ago
The pain's the same
Guess it never goes away
The water, the stars,
the moon, the trees
Are here with me
When no one else
Can seem to Be
The wind still dries my tears
After all these lonely years
The pain's the same
Guess it never goes away

c. 1992

Void

I push onward day after day
in the disguise of an automaton
trying to exist in some
predetermined reality
that is void of meaning until...
The occasional glimpse at the beyond
The brief excursions into mystery
that leaves my mind
spinning for days.
I derail from the mechanistic
track to find it difficult
co-existing with other robots.
Yet at moments of great depth,
when I come face to face with forever,
with greatness and splendor,
I shrink back and scramble
to find something, anything
that justifies my existence.
I dive into the ocean of human
Consciousness. I swim past
years of my life searching
for a shred of lasting meaning
a reason behind all the suffering
all the ecstasy and elation
the destitution in the everything
and the nothing that has
comprised my elusive life.
I submerge myself within
art of brilliant minds
gone before. I find no answer,
no permanence.
It's all swallowed up
into the blue-green wave
of oblivion. I emerge
empty handed with less
understanding than I had before
I took the plunge.
Everything is so permeable
dissolving in the swells of devouring time   c. 1995

Calm Storm

I am seeking truth in whatever form it may present itself.
I do not find the answers to my questions in this trivialized world as substantial as an umbrella in a hurricane.
I no longer seek shelter from that which is more powerful than me.
I am ready to be swept away in its torrents, to merge with the monster.
I am the hurricane and I am the building ripped to the ground by the force of my own will.
I build myself up only to tear myself down again, with each structure rising greater than the last, only to be destroyed again by a force of increasing strength.
It is part of the perpetual cycle that can be feared or embraced but cannot be avoided or ignored.
To shed the layers to reach the core is to die a thousand times, be a thousand times reborn into a form that's new.
It is to be filled with life and consent to death.
It is to be an angel in the depths of hell.
It is to be mortal and eternal at the same time.
It is to be everything and yet be nothing at all.
The world doesn't seem to care, but that's okay.
I exist nonetheless.

c. 1996

A part

I feel thoughts
           I think concepts
                      I know truths
           It's not about hunting it out
                 Or chasing it down
                           Forcing it into a structure
It's about opening our hearts
           Trusting our instincts
                      Pressing our palms against the Earth
It's about the way plants provide us with food and oxygen
                 And the way the sun heats
                           the surface of water
           It's not about defining it
                 Or labeling it or organizing it
                      or even understanding it
It's about knowing it by feeling it in the very
           molecular structure of our DNA
                      It's about seeing it
                           Really seeing it
                                 Embracing it
                                      Accepting it
                                           And changing it
                      When it cannot be accepted
           It's not about finding it
                 It's about allowing it to find us
It is the equilibrium
           The dynamics of internal and external
                                 Taking in and giving out
           It's about you
                 And it's about me
                      What it is to be together
                           What it means to be separate
                                 A part

c. 1993

Unclear

You're not who
you appear to be.
You're not the person
you think you are.
In a world that is
so unclear,
It is hard to be
Clear. Clearly.
You don't yet know
who you are,
who you really
want to be.
A little this way,
a little that.
Not as steady
on the inside
as the solid-seeming
outside. Still
caught in the web
of your own
thoughts. I feel
your projections
but these are not
close to my truths.
Do not be Confused.

c. 1995

Don't bother

Talking to me
With that condescending tone
As if I don't have the brain
To catch the concept on my own
Wasting your breath
Making yourself feel smarter
Explaining to me
How to be a self-starter
Based on your assumption
That I can't swim in the water
Like you're some kind of lifeguard
Motherfucker, don't bother
If you can't pay attention
Don't waste my time
If you can't see the situation
Don't act so sublime
It doesn't take much concentration
I have diagramed my mind
I straight up show you who I am
If you can't see me you are blind
Don't act so superior
I don't need no father
I never was your inferior
So brother, don't bother
Don't hang around with me
If you're not down with being real
It's important what you think
But you gotta show me how you feel
You can tell me that you're fearless
Yo, anyone can talk it
When your back's against the wall
I want to see if you can walk it
When nothing is in place
You have to try a whole lot harder
I understand busting your ass
But don't come at me like a martyr
If you can't hang with what you've chosen
Then why the fuck even bother
c. 1991

Disperse Attention

Way back in the day
you burned me at the stake
Today you burn me slowly
with the laws that you make
You make them so complex
make it hard to understand
so the mass is in the dark
while the few are in command
You say that I am free
but that's not really true
I'm free to think and act
in ways approved by you
When I express thoughts
that threaten your power structure
you silence my voice quickly
so your system doesn't rupture
You distract the population
with a commercial status quo
They buy it up not knowing
how much you're in control
So fixated on the money
they sacrifice their souls
striving hard to reach
elusive futile goals
while you pull the strings
and you set the traps
dispersing the attention
you keep it under wraps
A nation ruled by hypocrites
whose lives are fueled by fear
following false leaders
who are corrupt and insincere

c. 1990

Real Revolution

My strong opinions
they tend to offend
I say what I think
there's no time to pretend
I will not assert
that I go with the flow
see I am offended
by the status quo
can't stand how you treat me
like some stupid ho
'cuz boy I know things
you couldn't possibly know
It's sad that you hate me
because I am white
it's time we should learn
the things we should fight
Please don't despise me
because of my skin
Look past the surface
to what lies within
It's not about color
It's not about creed
It's about the oppression
and uncontrolled greed
while we are dividing
by gender and race
those in power destroy
what no one can replace
the longer we fight
amongst ourselves
the longer our power
decays on the shelves
The more time we waste
defining and labeling
the longer the lies
we continue enabling
We're still buying into
the concepts they sell
remaining entranced in

the synthetic spell
our intent stays unfocused
until we master our minds
and reject the mechanized
notions that blind
Time to face our own fears
and find our true source
realize revolution
is not about force
it's a deep transformation
that comes from within
we must know our selves
before real change begins
transmuting our ways
precedes changing the world
humans are like oysters
our souls are like pearls
if we're afraid to be real
and crack open our shells
we're simply more cogs
in an industrial hell
which is deadly to Life
like a cancerous cell

c. 1991

Narcissus

You think you're strong
You act so wise
You talk too loud
You drown their cries
You love your thoughts
You see yourself
Don't perceive beyond
to anything else
You do not listen
or look around
In your own reflection
someday you'll drown
Unless you open
up your mind
your own reflection
is all you'll find

c. 1988

Fool King

Your armor covers a crumbling interior
You try to project that you are superior
Your foundation is rattled to the core
This isn't your kingdom anymore
I doubt you will find more subjects to rule
The fool now the king, the king now the fool
Winds of fortune blow in another direction
The time has passed to make an objection
Your life has been fated by your ill doings
A humbler life you should be pursuing
Leave your castle and throne, just walk away
New lessons await you upon a new day
Search for the truth and seek to be wise
Earn forgiveness for your past lies
May you find peace and love in your heart
Then warring can end and healing will start

c. 1989

Watch the Weather

You judge me
according to your laws
the ones you created
the ones you uphold
I could be your princess prize possession
spread like a feast
for your consumption
I could consume your toxic teachings
or force my way to the top of your frail ladder
and try to make you think like me
I'd rather climb a tree
and assess all I can see
the fire the land the ocean the sky
You build bridges
connecting your empire with greed
I build your very cellular structure inside
I could be your brain surgeon
and dissect your pathologies
spread you thin under my microscope
and expose the very makeup of your material mass
like a dust bowl land raped of fertility
where nothing
the body the mind the heart the spirit
can survive
The times of turning are at hand
and false illusions can't sustain
deal the death card from the deck
and extinction is now
turn on the TV and try to turn it off
turn on the tap
and nothing comes to quench your thirst
to sustain your life
Stores lie empty as fields lie fallow
a responsibility
you could not possibly face
an evolutionary revolution
you could not possibly contain
you could not possibly control
as you wield the world apocalypse

I pray for future food
I pray for our flesh and blood
as you plague I heal
the East the South the West the North
the circle of life and the cross of suffering
the laws you don't understand
the balance you continue to deny
The limitation you try to ignore
is a venomous snake
waiting to bite beyond your antidote
and the storms of change are raging in

c. 1998

PART THREE

I moved swift and far across the gently sloping plains, leaping over excessively tall and sharp peaks, bouncing off the sculpted canyon walls of my youth. I sprinted to the outer boundaries of culture, not stopping to look back. I moved so far away from civilization central that it took a while for me to find my way back, when the time came that I wanted/needed to, (but that's another story…) I completely forgot to leave a trail of breadcrumbs, though they would've long since been eaten by the pesky tormenting magpies, by the time I finally returned.

If only someone would've taught me to drop pebbles…

Shortly after my release from confinement, I released myself from the confines of mainstream society. My experiences in the hospital solidified my sense that I could not trust outer authority and the cultural constructs they upheld. I knew in my bones that there was a higher order, a higher law, that ironically, I had access to deep inside myself. This was the gift of the initiation, the golden gift I brought back with me from the descent into darkness. I returned with golden wisdom, though I didn't really know it yet. My reentry into the world placed me into a wholly new place in society.

I entered fully into the external world of my choosing (or so it would seem). I left the arid land of my birth and struck out on a mythic adventure that was more magical, more filled with synchronicities, insights and awakenings than I could ever have imagined. My strange and spontaneous adventures stretched far beyond what I can begin to describe herein. I hope that the poems can adequately weave the storyline together.

Suffice it to say, I was initiated into the larger village as an unknowing keeper of an older knowledge, knowledge of an older way of being, of living closer to the bone, connected to the earth, standing outside of the cultural pattern far enough to see it more clearly. I honed my ability to see larger patterns at play, longer storylines in place. My view of the world expanded in ways it has taken me years to understand and integrate.

I packed my bags and stepped into a neo-tribal world of traveling revelers, dancing my way forward, learning to spin and twirl with my own capricious personality while trying to dodge the erratic hand of fate that opened doors one moment and smacked me to the ground the next. I hadn't known that the fates could be so fickle.

During my years of wandering, I learned to live at the crossroads with Hecate and her hounds. This venerable Greek crone taught me about the moon and her mysteries. She handed me keys and I unlocked doors to the realms of earth medicine and fairy magic. I learned about the healing herbs that graced the paths I walked and of the poisons that lurked in the shadows. Where others feared her, I took comfort in the ancient wisdom she generously doled out. I met others who fell under Hecate's spell. And under the silver light of the moon we conjured beautiful visions of cultural renewal growing out of the collapse and decay we smelled breeding in the darkness like fungi.

As I travelled the country and traversed the varied landscapes, I peeked into the assorted cultures they propagated. I become apprentice to Hermes - the cunning god of transitions, transgressor of boundaries, divine messenger and protector of travelers and thieves. I learned to wear many masks, according to the situation I found myself in. My shape-shifting abilities came in particularly handy many times. While I could don any persona that served me, I also continued courting my deeper, more authentic self, gently coaxing her to step forward and find expression in the poems and drawings I gushed like a newly tapped spring.

Untamed spirit
Wild fire soul
Lighting up the dark
Burning forests to the ground
Warm away the chill
Destroying everything in your path
Embers sweetly sting
Leaving ashes in your wake

I continued to roam, to connect and explore. I met Dionysus one night during a particularly raucous romp through the North Eastern woodlands. The lush forests seduced me into his inner circle. I thought it was my affinity for ecstatic states and mad revelry in the wilds that sealed my kinship with Dionysus. But it turns out that my intimacy with the ways of the mask formed a deeper bond that would resurface and command my attention many years later. I danced straight into Dionysus' exotic and at times dangerous world that lies beyond the known. At times, I nearly forgot myself in the frenzy of elation, but fate would inevitably bring me back with a hard slap of reality and I returned to my wounded and newly regrouping self over and over again.

I close my eyes
I feel the earth
Pulse below my feet
I feel the sky
Stretch above my skull
I draw it in from both sides
All sides, Inside, Outside
It's all relative
As it whirls and twirls
and mixes inside me
I have visions
Of underground caverns
Filled with virgin waters
And space stations
Like satellites
Orbiting planets
Unnamed by man
Worlds unknown
To this world
Words without sounds
I recognize
Resound in my head
And my tongue skews the language
I have not yet learned
As I try to put words to things
Beyond words
To ideas beyond thoughts
I am caught in my own web
And no expression is enough
I'm left with the mystery
Of that which can be experienced
But not explained
Some would say it is too hallowed

But I would never lock it in that box
It's not that simple
It's not that neat
Some things I cannot repeat
But I can transfer with my eyes
Or reveal in my step
But other things
Are for me to hold forever within
Maybe that's why
Some say these things are sacred

I eventually landed back in Colorado, tricked into coming home, it seemed. But I actually had an appointment with my own destiny, which I had entirely forgotten. I had a date with a dark-haired stranger who was fated to change my life forever.

SPRUNG

Dead Kids

Happiness is as elusive as shadows at sunset
That dance with the flashing neon signs
My vision is blurred by the dense fog collecting in my skull
The pounding rhythm of helicopter blades whirls in my head
The coarse pavement lies bitter beneath my flesh
I won't be going home again tonight

A distant echoing tune feels forced beneath my bleeding finger tips
My bowl is empty but nobody notices
Salty ocean air stings my nose
and the taste of fear burns the back of my throat
The bay feels colder when dead souls contort my thoughts
Turning fear sweet like candy at the circus

Childhood is a cruel joke on the spirit
The clowns weren't smiling because they were happy
The nasty wharf rats sharpen their tongues and their needles
We don't wear shoes because it is winter
The billboard says that youth is perfection
But the piercing sword of reality makes us hungry for tomorrow

I was content as a prison inmate
So I swam naked across the icy bay to let the magic potion fill my veins
Now I am peaceful and serene
And the silent music gathers at the base of my spine
The tight rope stretches narrowly before me
reminding me of a stolen youth
I drink the poison so I can be pure
No comprende Amigo
The curves in the highway are telling me it's time to go
The circus tents are collapsing around me

c. 1995

Finding Keys

Standing in the rain
Remembering the pain
Seeds planted in my head
Roots down to the dead
Forget about unending sorrow
Think about a new tomorrow
See the kids spin up and down
Dancing to the funky sound
Blue moon rising on the hill
Twinkling in the tiny pill
Capsule to the underground
Rattle and shake those bones around
A magic bus to shifty dreams
With talking trees and laughing streams
Mystery doors to other worlds
Hiding wisdom's veiled pearls
Concealed in the universe
Resounding in the music verse
Alight in every brilliant star
A voice exclaiming from afar
Winding from the river bend
spiraling headlong without end
Leave this world to take the ride
Flow into eternal tides
Thumping pulse beneath my feet
Guides me to the primal beat
Where oneness awaits at the gate
holding the measure of my fate

c. 1989

The Wave

Dive down deep
Spiraling towers of the sea
Come up for air
In the middle of the market
Big fish little fish
Dancing to calypso
Under the burning moon
The man in the suit
The tension in the air
Taste the poison
Beside the crashing waves
On the magic green carpet
Where camels drift
After the rain storm
On a high mountain vista
Beneath the ancient stars
Interlocking through time
Walking through tunnels
In the dark corridors of the brain
Listening to Bob Marley
Puffing like a dragon
Walking up the clown's tongue
Swinging from mossy locks
Fatter than a spleef
In the store with the red door
And the shiny black cats

c. 1990

I Am Your Government

I push cocaine in the cities to keep you under control.
My T.V. takes the place of your mind that I stole.
I tell you what to think: What is right; What is wrong.
I suck the free will out of you to make myself strong.
I cover up reality with a network of lies.
I deafen your ears to the sound of your own cries.
I teach you that difference is what you should fear,
So when the truth is spoken, you will not hear.
My greed is so far reaching, I always want more.
You fund the deaths of your own sons I kill in my wars.
My only fear is those whose minds and spirits are free.
They may wake you from deep sleep, open your eyes to see.

c. 1990

This poem was written in 1990 when I was 19 years old, standing in Lafayette Park (Peace Park), Washington DC, across the street from the nation's capital. These words entered my awareness and I grabbed a pen and my journal in order to capture them.

Morningside

Outside the leaves change
Turn brown, shrivel
Return to the earth,
Another summer has passed
It all came and went so quickly
I had no time to realize and reflect
I have time now
Is it time for dinner?
Or is it time for sleep?
Every morning I awake
And wait for the time to sleep again
Time is distorted
We all just
Wait
In fear
Not willing to hang on
Afraid to let go
I keep myself here
Waiting

c. 1990

This poem was written in 1990 during a trip with a friend I met on the road to visit her grandmother in a nursing home in Philly. I was struck by the lifeless life being plodded through by the residents. So earie and sad to witness.

Magic Woman

Medicine magic witchy woman
black cloth on her head
Ratty pushed beneath her collar
Soul sister, winter's child
raven feather in her pocket
shakin' hips like maracas down the alley
Butterfly spit on the sidewalk
jivin' like a rooster
rattlin' sticks on the fence post
wakin' up sleepy souls
pourin' stew into their empty lives
rainbow stew with cat paws and insect eyes
potion for the dead spirits
reminds them of their earth mother
Back street swinging in the twilight
with drums to call the moon
laughin' like a waterfall
at the hokey neon lights
blinking out the final words
of a culture that is dying
She don't like it any way
so try again tomorrow
and don't forget to call her next time
she'll bring the milk and honey
to sweeten up the sadness
and drive the madness from your bones

c. 1990

Maya

you may wish to keep her for yourself
but she cannot be possessed
her spirit as free as fire
she can withstand any test
welcome her with kindness
she may rest and keep you warm
then winds of change start blowing
and she's gone with the next storm
you need not try to follow her
she leaves behind no trail
her movements are invisible
when she shrouds them in her veil
she's elusive as the rainbow's end
her soul cannot be chained
enclose her in your fortress
but nothing you have gained
for once you think she's captured
she slips out under the door
she's gone before you notice
you won't see her anymore
do not try to entrap her
or keep her under glass
she'll dissolve into a shadow
and ooze out of your grasp
she will surely find you
if you're worthy of her trust
she'll share some of her secrets
but when it's time to go she must
it is no use to chase her
she'll leave no prints to track
she departs without a warning
not pausing to look back

c. 1990

Tear Stained

Tear stained eyes like bougainvillea
in the Andalusian sun
the wind bites cold and bitter
as it did when I was home
the sands have changed their color
the earth below has stayed the same
my life the sad blue sky
hangs heavy over me today
the joyful mocking flowers
replace the concrete in my sight
but the dark and restless dreams
still wake me in the night
the fears have changed their surface
like a snake shedding its skin
but the texture underneath
becomes coarse and rough again
I transform my thoughts of sorrow
like an alchemist of the soul
but beneath the gilded cover
lies the blackness as before
I have sought the words of wise men
learned the lessons of the babes
drowned my heart in freezing waters
purged my mind in burning flames
it seems nothing will relieve me
of this unrelenting pain
I try hard to forget them
but the memories remain
of shadows in the sunlight
and splinters in the flesh
this life laid out before me
is a never ending test

c. 1998

Diverging Days

Some days
I feel on top
Determining, deciding
Other days
I feel lost, confused
Just a pawn
In a game
Far out of my scope
Some days
I feel no ground
beneath my feet
Other days
I feel deeply
rooted in the Earth
Some days
I flow with the cycles
Step with the rhythms
Other days
I resist them
And wander amiss

c. 1992

Watcher

All I can do is watch
  as you pass
        with your common place clothes
            and your incomprehensible tongues
Your words are unfamiliar
  but your lives are not
            so strange
        to one who has been
behind palace walls and
        under city bridges
I can read your faces
  like books in
        my own language
I can feel your passions and
  sense your hidden fears
this brings me closer
  to a world
        so far
            from my reach
I cannot tell you
  where I have been or
        describe the things I love
All I can do is watch
  and listen
        to your unfamiliar words

c. 1998

White Wash

Beneath the beautiful white washed
exterior of purity
lies the crumbling truth of decay
and the darker reality of
impermanence and despair

The vibrantly illuminating patterns
cloak the central core of
unfulfilled desires and
fears like a plague
looming in the shadows

Dressed in the prophetic
robes of poverty
eyes darkened by experience
radiating knowledge of
the coin that has two sides

To have a pen is to have a voice
To have a dream is to have a vision
To have a purpose is to have a responsibility
To know the truth is to know the lie

The scent of saffron and ginger
The odor of olives and pescados
The awareness of the emptiness
comes before the filling up

The bright sunlight warms
the passing Moroccan hillside
Memories of terrain navigated
and strengths gained
For every pain endured
a lesson learned

c. 1998

Deep South

It's there in cane fields
The air thick with greed
Where the rising heat
Smells dirty and worn
Like a dollar bill

And at the tree farms
Where the only life
Is slaves and briars
And old memories
Rusting in a ditch

The city bleeds dry
Dreams of equality
With blacks to one side
And Cajuns in swamps
Whites go where they please

The old narrow streets
Seep with red velvet
And liquor stained love
And music is hot
Like cayenne pepper

See the local girls
Dance the zydeco
Like venomous snakes
In their high heeled shoes
Waiting to catch you

Among cypress trees
Where voodoo priestess
Hides behind her spell
When the drums silence
And the moon turns black

They watch for cages
Made of twisted vines
From bigoted pasts
And times forgotten
By those in power

Politicians smile
Hiding whips and chains
Behind their white backs
Declaring their god
Ruler of all men

c. 1996

Badlands

Fire spears from heaven
Pierce the night
Scorch the earth
Red as blood of pain
Stand in silence
The tale told
Spears fears tears
Beckoned to descend
Pulsing drum
Rhythmic chant
Legacy in rebirth
Warriors of peace
Howling wolf
Gentle wind
Speak without words
We are torn away
With beating hearts
Quickened pace
Primal friend
lead the way
Where danger passes
ancients are reborn
with songs of praise
to spirits of the land

c. 1990

Santa Nada

Running down
the road legends
buried back at camp
The desert is dry
No water tonight
No agua mi amor
Diablo afoot
recasting us into
ceremonial casualties
acculturated sorrow
We are stones in the
dried up river bed
stars in the sky
silence in the wood
pounding cadence
of our human hearts
The human heart lives
and dies as the wind
shapes the landscape
The stars appear fixed
but nothing is enduring
not forever
Nada mi amor
Not even stars

c. 2002

PART FOUR

In my early twenties I found myself stumbling blindly into uncharted and unforeseen territory. Before I knew it, the hand of fate had swooped in again to seize my life, freeze my plans and carry me off to a deeper stratum of initiation into womanhood. I found myself abruptly surrendering my winged shoes to pick up Cinderella's broom and become well versed in ashes.

This fragment of my story began, as many do, with love. Oh, love, the great paradox. To be swept up and swept away with a stroke of fate so powerful it can and does alter storylines forever. I was stung by one of Eros's indiscriminate arrows and my life would never be the same. This knock on my door brought some of my most significant lessons and two of my greatest teachers in the form of two sons that came into my life with godspeed.

It seems I had fallen in love with a dangerously charming *puer aeternus*, an eternal youth who turned out to be a rogue spirit in league with a band of scoundrels. Living outside the rules of proper conduct, doing whatever he pleased, the attraction proved in the long run to be an entirely unmanageable and ill-fated match. While the persona of the bandit who fancies himself a hero holds a certain magnetizing allure to a trickster girl like me, the shine quickly tarnishes. The glamour (as in spell) lifted when the house lights came up and the actors were seen without their make-up and costumes. Ah, just a bunch of boys who never grew up - Peter Pans with their Tinkerbells. I realized very quickly that, while I have my spritely ways, I am certainly no Tinkerbell.

I have returned from the bowels of the beast to take back the life you stole from me.

I was lost on your stormy sea but now I'm back to gather myself up.

I see how you've mistreated me
And left me feeling defeated
You repeatedly abused my love
Refused the gifts I offered
Filled your coffers by looting me
You stole the best parts of me
Ripped away the very heart of me
Your pillage left me scarred

The hand of fate is fickle. I repeatedly fell out and in, in and out of love. I was heart-broken, heart-breaking, tangling my life with the dramas that come from attractions and affections of the heart. So much fodder for the poetic temperament. While the scenes of love and betrayal played out on the side stage, a more lasting story strand was deftly spun around the main stage of my personal comedic tragedy.

My primary role became caretaker for my children. I never saw myself as maternal, but the instinct kicked in hard and I became a fierce mama lion protecting her cubs. I sent the lost boy back to Neverland and took up residence with my inner Mother. I deferred all decision-making powers to her and she would have me put my sons before all others. They occupied so much space in my heart, I wasn't sure there was room for another male energy in my life. Besides, I had fallen in league with my own inner Medusa, "Queen of Darkness and Generation," and under her tutelage, I became adept at turning men to stone with my deadly stare.

As the story goes, Medusa was once a golden-haired maiden who had the great misfortune of being fancied by the wrong man, or in her case, a god. One day Poseidon, Greek god of the sea, caught sight of Medusa in the marketplace. In a fit of greedy lust, he seduced her into Athena's sacred temple where he proceeded to rape the innocent and unsuspecting maiden. Athena returned and was appalled at the scene which she felt defiled the consecrated ground dedicated to her god(dess)liness. In a fit of rage she cursed Medusa, turning her lovely locks into serpents and her gaze into a weapon. And just like that, Medusa went from maiden to monster at the cruel hands of the gods.

Though I spent considerable time roaming my home city as Medusa cursed, I eventually came upon one who was particularly skilled with mirrors. Instead of beheading me, as many before him attempted, this one steadily held my reflection. Unafraid of my penetrating gaze and the crown of vipers I displayed, he persisted. He saw beneath the surface into Medusa's deeper origins as a serpent queen of an ancient Libyan tribe of female warriors. He helped me break the curse, flip the script, and return to more hospitable regions. In this chapter of my life, it was love that first bound me and it was love that eventually arranged for my release.

SPRUNG

Riddle of an Ancient Goddess

Will you know me
when I come
stretching silently
across the midnight sky
yesterday's dreams
tangled in my hair
the sweet scent of rain
on my whispering breath
held beneath my smile
coiling like a snake
waiting to strike
Will you know me
when you hear my cries
roaring like thunder
in the angry heavens
drowning the voices
of hatred and oppression
beneath my crashing waves
then growing gentle
like the wind through the trees
quietly chiming a forgotten story
to whoever is listening
like an invisible thief
hiding in the crevices
waiting to leap out
and pierce the silence
with a single note
from a songbird's throat
Will you know me
when you look
to the crimson clouds
for concealed wisdom
and to the orange moon
like beeswax melted warm
into the curves of the goddess
of cinnamon and myrrh
draped in the fragrant perfume
of chamomile flowers
leaving the sweet taste

SPRUNG

of honey on your lips
Will you know me
when I come
cutting the night
with a fiery sword
twisting shadows
into shiny gold rings
molding my fears like soft clay
at the hands of a sculptor
into radiant visions
of jewels like colored glass
reflecting ancient legends
and mysteries untold

c. 1996

Familiar Stranger

I see your god-like stature
more real than jaded gypsies
against a row of nuclear diviners
glowing in the aftermath radiation
of my shadowed midnight dreams
an attraction obscure as an
inter-dimensional vision that
draws me out into the moonlight
to count extinguished stars
and to revel in insomniatic madness
trying to grasp at the mirage
of this primordial landscape circus
screaming into the oblivion of
the stellar vortex void
my soul is a serpent
twisted into mandallic patterns
you stretch across your back
I wander through the venusian sound waves
to find impressions of wild rhapsody
and your sunbeamed apparition
among convoluted cages of false meaning
I articulate my enigmatically enchanting delusions
and momentarily infiltrate your fluctuating reality

c. 1990

Soul Gazers

Shape changers Soul gazers
Will we be the ones
To bring our songs of spirit
Share our thoughts of things to come
Join beyond the boundaries
When we hear the call of time
Place our hearts into the fires
Forging strong and wild minds
Will we find ourselves as champions
With refinements strange and fair
Remembering mad confusion
Seeing truth behind a stare
As we cry when life has fallen
Shout out when ignorance reigns
Learn to understand our callings
And recognize our pains
We dream of vast tomorrows
And imagine peacefulness
We stand and face life's sorrows
Yet still know true happiness
Possessing priceless wisdom
Retaining treasured keys
We choose our destinations
Fashion new realities

c. 1990

Enveloped

Enveloped in indigo we walk together
Venus rising to the beat of the drum

Laughing eyes reflect gemstone dreams
Winging lights waltz on leaves in the mist

We speak in gentle whispers
trying to forget the pain at our feet

Entrancing stares invite aching smiles
But fear of love splits the path

Our souls cry out as we turn away
Heartsongs left unsung

c. 1990

Amore

From out of the silent oneness
The song of love did start
Melody became the mind
Rhythm became the heart

Your smile unlocks the chamber
To find my treasure whole
Your voice echoes songs long past
Your eyes reflect my soul

Hand of time pulls us apart
We learn so as to grow
Then our songs will become one
Life's secrets we shall know

c. 1992

Crushed

I painted you visions
Intricate and fragile
As a dragon fly wing
And whispered secrets
Like a moonless night
With a thousand crickets
Singing sadly to the wind
Your deeds were careless
Like icy cold waves
Slapping the side of a boat
Your distant demeanor
Pierced like a shard
broken glass against supple skin
Shattering sweet illusions
Bleeding fiery passions dry

c. 1995

Over

I didn't want us to end this way
I loved you as life itself
Unable to stay, you turned away
Left me struggling by myself
It blows my mind a love so strong
Could vanish into to dust
I spent my days not letting go
But now I know I must
A broken heart and shattered world
Haunts me as this ends
Now we're apart, the dream of Us
Is scattered to the wind

c. 1996

Paper Doll

I'm feeling rather used
but this isn't the first time
you call me when it suits you
leave me hanging on the line
by now I should expect it
it's far from fresh or new
leaving me with nothing
is like a game to you
I'm the fool to let you in
whenever you desire
trying to be with you
is like walking a high-wire
with every single step
there's fear that I may fall
then you can peel me off the floor
and paste me to your wall
the flattened out remainder
of my true identity
the shell of my full being
is all you seem to see
I feel as if I'm played with
like a heartless, mindless toy
wasting my affections
on a narrow-minded boy

c. 1996

Snake in the Grass

I hope you like my house
my children and my man
I hope you're feeling comfortable
with your little plan
You can't hide your intentions
I will always understand
You cannot erase me
Try to replace me if you can
He will always love me more
because I'm the one who's wise
You're stronger than I expect
If you can look me in the eyes
I imagine you'll shrink back
when I return to town
But I will not attack
I know my place upon this ground
I advise you to be careful
Watch that you do not fall
when you learn you are no more
than just a lesson to us all

c. 1997

Double Take

Avoiding the crude and distorting lens of my reality, I snake through the cold city streets like a viper. Avoiding the snap-shot scenarios, I slip into the cracks in the sidewalk.

You dance her to my door as if I have no sense. As if I do not feel the stabbing stare of your eyes through my soul like a dull and rusty knife. As if I can simply trade away my disastrous desires for desolate days of discontent and not feel the load it has left me. Like I can fill the devouring dark with your droning depictions of ever-changing whims and silently keep your secrets forever. Ignoring my emotions, you trample them freely under your heaving remorse in order to spare her fragile magazine cover ego. As if I am the strong one who can afford the freeze-frame feelings of fickle-minded affairs.

The city streets dim as the shutter closes on her naive notion and dangling dream to frame you in her fanatic schema - Trying to keep you from wandering the scope of your out-of-focus fancies which direct you to my doorstep and draw you back to hers. As if you have regard for no one. As if you are obliged to none. So I carefully filter my reactions and consciously develop my character, as she exposes hers, and you clumsily attempt to conceal yours.

Avoiding the crude and distorting lens of my reality, I snake through the cold city streets like a viper. Avoiding snapshot scenarios, I slip into the cracks in the sidewalk...

c. 1997

Time to Learn

Who do you think you are
And who do you think I am
Time to show me some respect
I won't explain this all again
If it wasn't for your mama
You wouldn't be here today
Stop looking at my body
Hear the things I have to say
If you strip me of my dignity
To hang me on your wall
You will miss something of value
And neglect to see your fall
If you keep going forward
Trampling women as you climb
Your lusty low ambitions
Will poison heart and mind
Leave you bemused and blind
I embody ancient wisdoms
My powers are quite real
I can help you find your spirit
And teach your heart to feel
I can expose all of your wounds
And show you how to heal
But as long as you play games
Pretending to be king
Your delusion will remain
And you won't learn a thing

c. 1993

Arrogant Heart

An arrogant heart
    Can never understand
The deep rooted wisdom
    Of a compassionate man
You can know many people
    Yet still feel alone
You may live in dwelling
    Yet never feel at home
You can hear someone's thoughts
    Yet not know their mind
You may have things in common
    Yet not be their kind
If you play childish games
    Be aware what you do
You will find you harm others
    And destroy what is true
If you keep yourself distant
    Stay removed and unaware
People may think you're gifted
    But they won't really care
Beware of fooling yourself into
    Believing you're the king
And not a fool who is smaller
    Than his majestic dreams
Keep everyone away
    And someday you'll find
You won't fill your heart
    By feeding your mind

c. 1995

Waiting

Sitting by the window
waiting for night to come
The street lights up before me
I feel I've just begun
I'm not sure what awaits me
I feel shadows closing in
Am I facing my next lesson
or escaping once again?
It's said for every pleasure
you have to pay a price
Is there truth within that
or is it misguided advice?
Why do I have to learn things
the hard way for myself?
Can't let my dreams extinguish
or sit dusty on a shelf
Sometimes I think I'm running
from demons in my head
forgetting what I've been through
regretting what I've said
I feel the time is coming
to stand and face my fears
without a hand to help me
or dry away my tears
No one else can save me
It's me I have to face
before I'll be unburdened
and get out of this place

c. 1997

Coffee Shop Thoughts

I see your sad brown eyes
dark as the coffee in my cup

My hands are shaking
and my wooden chair is hard

Someday I'll rest on soft grass
Someday you'll understand

The city exposes me like an x-ray
I have a heart beneath my chest
Sometimes it makes me lonely

I want to kick the walls down
and watch you float into a sky
That isn't choking with pollution

I want to look out the smoke stained windows
And smile at the weeds pushing
through the cracks in the sidewalk

Maybe that will teach them
Maybe someday they will learn
when their bulldozers die
and frustrated angels find their wings

I would take you with me
If you found wings of your own

c. 1997

Watch Me Bleed

You watch me bleed
You see me standing here in need
but you watch me bleed
you never seem to hear my plead
You just watch me bleed
           watch me bleed
                 watch me bleed
Can you hear me crying?
When I say it's breaking me
You know that I'm not lying
It's a heavy load
Can't you see me trying?
I see you dig my grave
As you watch me dying

You just watch me bleed
you see me standing here in need
But you watch me bleed
You never seem to hear me plead
So just watch me bleed
           watch me bleed
                 watch me bleed
It's wearing on my soul
  And it makes me tired
It's severing my goals
  It leaves me uninspired
It suffocates my dreams
  And stifles my desires
I'm choking on the smoke
  I can't put out the fire

You just watch me bleed
you see me standing here in need
But you watch me bleed
You never seem to hear me plead
You just watch me bleed
           watch me bleed
                 watch me bleed
c. 1995

Content Alone

Lightning strikes outside my window
As the rain comes pouring down
I don't mind being alone tonight
Knowing you're out on the town
As the years have passed between us
I've changed the way I see
I'm not controlled by my emotions
Not so attached to you and me
The wind howls upon my doorstep
As I sip hot herbal brew
Remembering how my visions
Always centered on me and you
Now my sight's on the horizon
Drawing me out to the unknown
As I close some doors behind me
I face my destiny all alone
If I hadn't the strength inside me
I wouldn't walk this rocky road
My dreams are sent to guide me
To lighten up this heavy load
So I accept the tasks I'm given
Transcending struggle and the fight
As I blow out the final candle
I'm content alone tonight

c.1997

Nameless Inspiration

I know you're not in love with her
it echoes in your sighs
you're longing for your freedom
it escapes out of your eyes
I know you have to stay there
and tend the seeds you've sown
and I am bound to stay here
I have seedlings of my own
last night I dreamt your colors
and your sweet angelic face
somehow we are connected
but for now there is no place
I would not betray her
or draw you from her side
I'll turn the other way now
and keep my thoughts inside
I'll forget about your smile
and I'll erase your voice
I'll focus on myself now
it seems the wisest choice
Someday it may be different
Perhaps we'll meet again
a nameless inspiration
is all you'll be 'til then

c. 1998

Still I Wait

I wait for you
who may never come
with pen in hand
writing away the days
that are the pages
in the book
that is my life
staring at the portrait
of a life that I have painted
with concentrated strokes
traveling over waters
bluer than jewels
in an Egyptian crown
watching people living lives
never knowing what it means
to be alive
aware of every breath
as I travel over mountains and plains
catching every color
of every wild flower
in the snare of my eye
filing them away for future fields
on the canvas of other worlds
that dwell only in my dreams
searching the eyes of strangers
for the spark of knowledge found
and mysteries understood
for reminders of
the one I don't remember
the one I can't forget
who comes to me in dream-time
yet eludes me when I wake
So I dance under the starlight
stroll foreign beaches all alone
I laugh and cry and die
a thousand deaths within my heart
waiting for you
who may never come
c. 1998

Who I Am

I'm feeling
things I can't explain
And I am listening to your heart
Beating in my brain
And I am trying
Not to scare you away
Because I'm tired of being alone
And I want you to stay
But I'm not perfect
And I need you to see
I am afraid and sometimes mean
And I'm not everything I seem
I have told my share of lies
And I've betrayed people I've loved
Sometimes I'm more like a vulture
Than a peaceful little dove
But I am trying
to show you what's real
And I can pause my thoughts
To find out how you really feel
And I will listen
And I'll try to understand
And if you don't expect too much
I'll show you who I really am
Even though this world
Seems to bring out my worst
Sometimes it saturates me
Until I feel like I'll burst
But I want you
I need you to comprehend
that I've never had anything
on which I could depend
That's why I'm armed
and I'm ready to defend
my own tiny plot of truth
where I can be just who I am

c. 2001

Confessions

What if I told you
I never want to be without you
I want to spend my days
gazing into lush green
jungles in your eyes
I want to feel your breath
like the petals of an orchid
raise the hair on my skin
as we begin to live out
conversations we have
with our minds

In the early morning dream-time
I trace the outline of your body
like intricate patterns of light
with the tips of my fingers
As you pull me in tighter
I fall into fertile fields
I walk your winding paths
enter a domain where I could remain
forever in the folds of your skin
never again surrender
to the demands of the day

c. 2002

Water Woman

If I were a river
and you were a stone
I would wash my body
against your surface
make your rough edges smooth
I would allow myself
to evaporate in
constant repetition
so I could precipitate
down and down again
give myself to you
in the form of a thousand tiny drops
each containing, reflecting
the full spectrum of light
seep into your crevices
drip from your edges
condense myself
around you
engulf you in
elemental truths
as I crash against your core
before rising up slowly
drop by drop
until you know me only as a trickle
as a cloud in the sky
hovering, waiting
to rain myself down on you
again and again

c. 2002

Simple Desires

I just wanted
to love you
in a simple way
Like a raindrop
falling from a cloud
Not thinking
how it's falling
Not wondering
nor worrying
where it will land
Like a butterfly migrating
across continents
with no map
no compass nor guide
knowing where it's going
by instinct alone
But the world around me
shuns simplicity
mistaking it for stupidity
or laziness
In its dazed state
the world enforces
arbitrary complexity
like it's the only noble
Way to be
to think, to live, to love
Forces outside of me
force me incessantly
to question you
to question me
to think, think, think, think, think
Until my head becomes ruler
and my heart converts to subject
Subjected to distortions
Measured out by mind
My mind, their minds
the mutually paired mind
of despair, jealousy, fear
Until nothing is clear

and my affections
become the trending
topic of conversations
I have no say in when
I just wanted
to love you
in a simple way
without the need
for text book explanations
calculated configurations
a breakdown
of gains and losses
a spreadsheet
mapping my emotions
leading me to draw
bottom line conclusions
as a graphic depiction
This addiction is not mine
This is not my line of viewing
My lines are not divisions nor
increments on rulers
My lines do not partition
They form curves and angles
that meet to form pictures
and words without summations
Because I have no need for
bottom line assumptions
I've no use for such illusions
My lines are simply edges
where shadows adjoin light
marking time to place
mind on hold making
space for heart
and extending it the right
to simply feel as it will

c. 2002

Nobody's Son

Stormy ocean eyes
Take in tiny grains of sand
Banded to sinking shore lines
Fearing the undertow
But yours is not to be washed away
As legends of annihilates
Infiltrate the cracks on the ceiling
Your third eye links to mine
Revealing the truth
That your up and coming is assured
As ripe fruit falls
To the force of gravity
And I have in me the ability to see
Opulent jade treasures
Where other pleasure seekers
Only find the grit on the surface
Area of an hourglass face
The time measurer turns
Obscuring subtle grace and charms
As the full becomes empty
the empty becomes filled
And the buried is unveiled
As the final grains fall
Yours is the stalk ready for harvest
The reaper not yet come
The keeper of your heart's interest
You hold in the palm of your hand and
I am the one who spins straw into gold
Like a fiery orb in the heavens
You transverse celestial years
The rest of your fears ablaze
I attest to our origins as you gaze into
My deep-space lunar rhythms
Oscillating to your jungle beats
Souls meet rising and setting
As we circle around truth
With centrifugal intensity
And this city is lost in the vacuum
Of our remote control memories

As our roots touch the Earth's core
No more shall we suffer
From the pesky bits of falsities
Stuck between our well-rehearsed smiles
That after a while make our jaws sore

c. 2002

Love Uprising

All I ever wanted
was to spend forever
in your embrace
To erase our fears
and replace them with love
and funky baselines
keeping time with
the rhythms of the globe
But we must first find
our gorgeous minds open
when all of the signs
in all of the windows
scream Closed
Where no one knows
if we'll ever be able
to buy food in cans again
When the end is the beginning
of a new way of being
Where seeing is the only sense
revealing the non-sense
the absence of reason
and the treason we commit
on this earth every day
All I ever wanted
was to birth a new empire
that inspires the need for no rules
or false boundaries
Only foolish revelry
And the things we need to survive
Where everyone is alive with knowing
of how to grow utopia on the tree
like it's the only fruit worth picking
Because sacrifice is no longer in fashion
and passion is the fuel
propelling us into a prosperity
where our memories of suffering
are fairly forgotten
amid the honeyed symphonies
we belt out in harmony

as we securely join hands
across the borders of eternity
moving beyond imperfect perceptions
of rhyme and time and space
replacing them with the sublime
and in time with higher love
then combine all the above with
divine understanding

c. 2003

Oh Baby

You got me thinkin' thoughts
I haven't had before
Like how to drag you from that chair
Down to the floor
And all the things that I could do
To make you beg for more
How I could melt you down and rock you
To your core

The way you look at me
I can read your mind
I feel your thoughts creeping up on me
From behind
I can give it to you raw
Or I can be refined
But what I got in store for you
Cannot be defined

I'm the definition of the phrase the bomb
I can infiltrate your brain like I'm an intercom
And if you don't resist my touch
I'll hold you in my palm
Cuz baby I can be your storm
And I can be your calm

I know that you can tell
That I'm not like the rest
I'm the genie in the lamp
Awaiting your request
So if you dare to dip your hand
Into my treasure chest
You won't believe all the things
We can manifest

c. 2001

SPRUNG

TINA AZARIA

PART FIVE

My return to the high city on the plains was one of mixed blessings and mingled emotions. I had a deep appreciation for my natural surroundings, for the spirits of the land and my own ancestral roots which together helped hold my soul in place while life spun like a tornado around me. At times, I could barely manage to keep my bearings. But somehow I advanced myself and the two dear souls I was entrusted with.

Beyond romantic love, other enduring story threads created the weft of motherhood and the warp of sisterhood that wove structure and texture into my daily life. Peter Pan had long since landed himself in prison, leaving me the sole captain in charge of the mother ship. It was another mixed blessings, which I in time learned to navigate more gracefully. The plight of single motherhood is no joke. It colored my perceptions of and experiences in the officious world and added fuel to my trickster-rebel spirit. For a time I became a more persistent social and environmental activist, until the dysfunction and in-fighting sapped my inspiration and drive. As I struggled to support myself and my young sons, I was also blessed to study fine art, martial arts, healing arts and to work as a writer.

During this time of my life, the challenges were many, yet so were the gifts. Every time I began building up hubris, I was broken to pieces and reminded to remain humble and in service to something higher than my own ego. Though it was at times excruciating, I now thank "the powers that be" for so reliably schooling me at every turn. Like in the poetic tale of Inanna, Sumerian "Queen of Heaven," I was never simply let off the hook until I had adequately hung in a suspended, reflective state, staring down my own inner Ereshkigal, Queen of the Under World, who systematically stripped me at every initiatory gate before dismembering me completely.

> This life is trying to suck me dry
> Suck me dry and drain me
> I have no more tears to cry
> I am becoming a desert
> A waste land
> A rag that has been used too many times

To clean up too many messes
Thread bare
With nothing to spare
Soil that is leached
The beach of a lake that has evaporated
A lease to a dream that has terminated
A field that has been harvested too many times
I am a fire extinguished
A desire outgrown
An unknown solution
To a well-known problem
That has been cleared from the closet
And hauled away as rubbish
Too soon
Before the sorting took place

I was fated to endure a debilitating injury that left me bed-bound for months and taught me profound lessons in the art of surrender. I had already been through a painful divorce, which later landed an unexpected and exasperating custody litigation on my doorstep and brought my inner warrior front and center. I fought and I won, but it cost me plenty. My resources were tapped continuously until my well appeared to be dry.

I was wrung through life's wringer too many times. Threadbare, I feared I would disappear. But I instead learned that my sons and I are more sturdy and resilient than I had previously imagined. In time, I came to accept that change is the only constant and that death is innately and intricately woven into the very fabric of life. I was forced again and again to dismantle my life, brick by brick, to submit to a comprehensive unravelling each time I thought a weaving was complete.

I learned that as much as I am a creator, I am equally a destroyer. I awoke to the stark recognition that I had become an unwitting apprentice to the fates themselves. I was being educated by Clotho to spin the threads of my life. Like Lachesis, I too had to learn to measure, and like Atropos, to cut threads with proper discernment and resolve. Daughters of necessity, we learned to do as we must, my fateful sisters and I.

From that point on, I more consciously allowed myself to be instructed by my fortune and misfortunes. I began to divide my time equally between the palace of the Hindu goddess Kali (in all of her forms – Creator, Sustainer and Destroyer) and the temple of Kwan Yin (Guanyin), East Asian goddess of mercy and bodhisattva of compassion. With one hand I wielded a mighty sword, while I lit candles for peace with the other. I could not escape paradox, so I learned to embrace it as best as I could.

I spent many days, months, and years focused on healing the deeply entrenched stories of injury I wore like badges on my sleeve (when I wasn't hiding them under my pillow). I was a wounded warrior who had the good fortune of spending many nights circled with wise women around campfires and candle light crying, dancing and chanting our prayers to the divine mother in her many forms. I learned so much about the history of women, the myths, the stories and symbols of the feminine principle that were voraciously resurfacing and being restored to our culture. My affinity with the myths had to do with the way they resonated deep within my bones and reverberated through my psyche. They were in me and about me, inseparable from my personal experiences. I came to understand that the personal truly is universal.

One night, in the sacred circle, I was visited by Sophia, ancient Greek goddess of Wisdom. Her fragmented story of falling like a star from the heavens, to be trapped in darkness, before undergoing a lengthy process of redemption and finally ascension, touched my soul and continued to intrigue me for years. She is the bright shiny spirit trapped in matter – the materialization of spirit and the spiritualization of matter. Hers was one of the first stories of the fall followed by salvation. Many years later, I set out to excavate the shards of her story through a lengthy review of source texts. The exhuming of her story became a mirror for reclaiming my own.

Vast light
Veiled in darkness
Guide pilgrims' journeys
With starlit lantern

Across wide oceans
Wild deserts
And deserted hearts
Yawning and stretching
Around creation
As you awaken
Stir and rise
Wise one within

We all have stories. Many parts of my story I have largely resisted, loathed, and even feared. In moments of darkness I have found myself screaming up into the heavens "I don't want this story! I hate this story! I want a different story!" Yet, I continually return to a place of peace with this tale that I now wear like the ancient shaman's medicine mask. It is my story, yet it is only a story. It isn't who I am, not all of who am I. I see the archetypal patterns in my personal narrative and know that I am living a universal myth, one that has been playing itself out on the world stage for millennia.

Some days it is still difficult to carry this particular set of stories on my shoulders. But they are mine. No matter how hard I try or how much I wish to separate myself from them, they are mine to carry. In many ways I have transcended and moved beyond and out from underneath it all. But in some ways it still follows me like a shadow cast by my mere presence. Some days I stretch like a wildflower pulling in and synthesizing brilliant rays of sunlight. I celebrate the beauty of life with passion and gratitude. Other days I sink into the shadowy dark places in crevices and under rocks. I let the stories engulf me and grief washes over me like ocean waves. I breathe, move, paint and write the pain out of my heart and body. I don masks and dance my joy, my reverence, and my sadness in ritual frenzy. I look for the patterns and symbols that infuse my reality and connect me to the paradoxical collective human story of immense suffering and incredible ecstasy, and I am grateful for the golden soul that shimmers in the dark and continues to illuminate the path before me.

I am writing this letter to take back my life from the lie that threatens to devour it. Like a phoenix, I rise from the ashes of a life that has outgrown its usefulness. I am no longer a sad, scared, confused child. I am a grown woman, here to take back my power, the power you have tried so hard to wrestle away from me all these years.

The ancestral venom has not poisoned me, but has made me stronger, wiser, and clearer than I ever imagined. Every attempt to keep me down, to keep me quiet has failed. The mechanism has broken down, the chain cut, the lie penetrated, and the truth has finally been set free. I have entered the labyrinth and today I have reached the center. I slay the Minotaur and release myself from the fear and torment that has hung heavy over me.

The lie must die that the truth may be born. I am the gatekeeper. I am the gate. I am the one who must cross the threshold. I am the alpha, the omega. In me it began a thousand lifetimes ago. In me it ends today.

I can submit and be still no longer. The day of reckoning has come. I am like the Buddha, ten thousand angels to the left of me, thirty thousand to the right, twice that below me and innumerable above. And here I sit, beneath the great Tree of Life, on the Immovable Spot, where Time and Space no longer exist. I have separated myself from the world, penetrated a source of deep power. Now I must return with an offering. I offer up my words as swords of truth and prayers of healing. May that which is poisoned, dead and decaying be cut away, so that which is true and intact may live on in health, balance, and harmony.

Personal Journal Entry c. 2001

Beginning of All

To be pregnant
to grow life within my womb

The gateway to the world
is sacred, is magical
is the beginning of all we know

Without the mother there is none
All must pass through her gate
to enter life, to enter death

People have forgotten
to honor the great mystery of the Mother
Potent, radiant, she embodies
the creative forces of the universe

c. 1992

The Mother

The work of the mother is sacred, is vital.
In her, all life begins.
She links future to past.
Through her, life expands.
Without the shedding of her blood,
without the pain of her labor,
the wheel of life would cease to turn.

c. 1994

Sing Over the Bones

Tonight
I sing over the bones
Of my dreams
That died
When I became
Somebody's daughter
Somebody's wife
Somebody's mother
Tonight
I belong only
To the desert
To the Earth
Tonight
I belong to
A thousand stars
And the roundness
Of the moon
Tonight
I belong to
the Emptiness
Of my own womb
Where my dreams
Never die
But grow
Ever strong
Under my own
Watchful protection
To flesh out
When the time
And moon
Is ripe

c. 2000

Hear Me

Lead me gently
untie my hands
hear who I am
stop barking commands
don't blame your decisions
on a network of laws
designed to oppress
in the name of a cause
created by God or created by man
forcing me to conform
to a controlling plan
putting up fences
and drawing out lines
that do not protect
but restrict and confine
that sadden my heart
and stifle my mind
when wisdom and justice
grow harder to find
behind power and riches
the arrogant hide
creating great walls
of ignorant pride
locking the doors
with the world shut outside
fearing the truths
that are buried inside
of the ones left to suffer
the repressed, the denied
while the ones in control
contently reside
my struggle to survive
is shoved neatly aside
and the wrongs the rulers
to themselves won't confide
so the choices they make
are excused, justified
while my voice and my truth
are swept away in the tide   c. 1998

As a woman
    I have the power to change—again and again
        I possess the cycles of creation and destruction within
            I am ruler of my own body, my own life
                I wish to rule no others
As a woman
    I am one with the cycles of the moon
        I am daughter and keeper of the Earth and her creatures
            I am the gateway to life and therefore death
                In this third dimension
As a woman
    I have a truth that has been feared
        I have a power that has been oppressed
            I have vulnerabilities that have been exploited
            I have a voice that has been silenced
As a woman
    I hold the future birth of man in a very real way
        The choices I make affect the world around me
            I am rocking the boat, shaking the tree, turning the tide
                I am reclaiming my ancient powers
As a woman
    I have a strength no man can know
        I have an intimate understanding of the webs of connection
            I know the threads of life that bind us together
                And the secrets of the stars and stones
As a woman
    I have a wisdom that cannot be ignored
        I have a perspective that must be embraced
            I have the visions of healing and wholeness
                That is needed to evolve, or even to survive

c. 1999

Beauty Worship Cult (Venus Distorted)

How I look is important
because what I say is not
Worse than being mortal
I am woman
I bleed
I age
I give birth
to life's imperfections
Imperfection is sin
if I cannot be perfect
be beautiful
I should rather be invisible
or paint on product perfect
luminosity to hypno-trip
I must divide
and conquer
with my ephemeral external
physical presence
because my internal
intellectual glowing
spark of radiance
is immaterial to
publicly prescribed visions of
exalted angelic faces
of supermodel saviors
trying to keep me in line
behind the cosmetic counter
capitalist controllers
guardians of my beauty/value
I am sanctioned and separated by
deliberately disorienting
depictions of my body
down-casting my soul into
body bondage
enslaved to the doctrine of image
bound to the Beauty Book
like some divine pronouncement
I am ordained the omnipotent
queen of beauty's bounty…briefly

before reality renders me
flawed and shamed
into seeking salvation in a bottle
I am made up like a mascot
my material much too mass-ive
for marriage or money manifestation
starvation is the only purification
sinking into skeletal sanctity
my skin-shell is my protection
is my only passport
into the sacred inner
circle of obsession with
the formulated female form
society's vested interest in
woman as object
If I am not a textbook beauty
then what will save my soul
from the profane sin
of unregulated ugliness
or the condemnation of mediocrity
What am I
if I am not beautiful?

c. 1999

Sedna

I was betrayed
By patriarchy's lie
With salty tears
My eyes reddened
I am Sedna
Goddess of the deep
Keeper of the tides
Tempest queen
Hurricane mama
The ocean my grave
Emotions Wash over me
Nothing can save me
From the storms to come
Cursed with beauty
They pursued me
Self-possessed
I accepted no man's offer
To be contained
I remained free
Until the bird man
Came to take me away
He swayed me with promises
Not to be kept
I was swept away
Into filth and squalor
Enslaved was I
No one to save me
Until my father
Arrived to fetch me
Trying to catch us
The bird man chased me
To save his own skin
My father forced me
Down into the icy sea
I clung to the boat
He severed my fingers
Flung his oar into my eye
My blood pored
In waves it flowed

Into the blue
And I sank down
To the ocean floor
No more to see the sun
Left to die
Cast to the watery deep
I made the darkness my home
Alone and defeated
My cries became the
Songs of the wales
My fame grew
I became the subject
Of tales told by men
Of lovely mermaids
No human could hold
They told stories of
how seals and dolphins
Fish of the sea
They come from me
From my severed limbs
They swim in me
I am the waves
Rolling onto the shores
I am more than
Any man can know
From my salty grave
I send forth life
To clothe and feed you
I need nothing
But humbly request
The blessing of respect
And the gift of gratitude

c. 2002

Mother Help Me

My heart cries out to you
Mother can you hear me

I wander through your woods today
as the tears roll down my face
although your beauty surrounds me
my sorrows I cannot erase
I reflect on my life by your waters
watch the patterns of clouds in the sky
then I go to deep places within me
and I lower my head as I cry

My heart cries out to you
Mother can you feel me

I sit by the banks of your river
rolling by me like clear crystal beads
try forgetting the hardships before me
I study the shapes of your weeds
I bend down with respect and honor
grasp a smooth river rock in my hand
try to gather up somewhere inside me
all the strength my life seems to demand

My heart cries out to you
Mother can you help me

c. 1998

Apathetic System

Apathetic system
bury me underground
when I push up to the surface
you try to beat me down
because I am a woman
because I have no wealth
you rape me of my power
stack me on a shelf
put obstacles before me
you hope I cannot meet
convinced of your control
expecting me to take defeat
that will never happen
your weakness makes me strong
I won't bow down to your structure
sit back and play along
despite your opposition
I will still succeed
and you will seek my wisdom
I have many things you need
deny the strength I harbor
but someday you must concede
my spirit is a flower
in your garden full of weeds
not just something pretty
you need flowers to have fruit
the inherent worth of women
is a truth you can't dispute
despite your dreams of glory
despite your quests for gold
my truths will grow around you
they're beyond your passing hold
I will be restored as equal
not above yet not below
we will find a place of balance
and a new dream we will sow

c. 1997

To My Sons

I'm sorry for all I cannot control
I wanted it perfect, it cannot be so
Still you will grow and wisdom you'll gain
with your own stories someday to proclaim
Your strength and resilience I daily behold
I watch in amazement as you unfold
Forever you will have a home in my heart
long after the day we finally part
We are deeply connected, it will always be so
For now I will teach you all that I know

c. 1997

Dreams

Don't let them tell you to
stop dreaming big dreams
Whoever says dreamers
are not realists
are profoundly mistaken
Everything we have
Everything we see
Everything created
was once a dream
in a dreamer's mind
divine or mortal
Dreamers who manifest
are indeed realists
of the most powerful kind
So dream your dreams forward
Let them shape you
from the inside out
give your most beautiful dreams
form and voice and vitality
Your dreams may one day
change the world
so nurture your dreams
like the rare seedlings they are
for one day we all may
rest in the shade of
your resilient dreams

c. 1997

Sister
Sister, my sister
stay for a spell
you seem a bit troubled
as if things are not well
let's go for a walk
in this beautiful weather
you know if we talk
we both will feel better
all we can do when
the world's treating us wrong
is not let it taint us
but make us both strong
when we start to feel
shoved to the ground
all we can do
is turn it around
pick ourselves up
and hold it together
and search for a way
to make it all better
if it seems like there's nothing
that you can do
come and find me
and I'll try to help you
when no one can hang
with the life you have chosen
don't let it jade you
or make your heart frozen
although it's a struggle
these lives that we live
we can't turn away
we have so much to give
sometimes it may feel like
we're stuck on our own
but we cannot forget
we're not really alone
we have Mother Earth
and the sky up above
and the beautiful blessing
of sweet sister love   c. 1996

Release

I release the shame
Of the one who feels broken
The parts that seem
Vulnerable, ugly and weak
I release the blame
From the one who's been wounded
The parts that feel
Dreadful, disheartened, and beat
I release the stains
On the one who's been shattered
The parts that are
Damaged, faulty and streaked
I release the fears
From the one who feels fragile
The parts that seem
Tired, flimsy and creased
I release the ire
In the one who's been slighted
The parts that hold
Judgment, confusion, defeat
I call in the hope
For the one who has courage
The parts that are
Candid, assertive and clear
I call in the faith
Of the one who's awakened
The parts that
Forgive, expand, persevere
I call in the love
For the one who's arisen
The parts that are
Sacred, exquisite, revered

c. 2001

Reminder

I am you
I am your dreams
I am the voices of your ancestors
singing and dancing from across the great sea
I am here to remind you to remember
to re-member yourself
to call forth all the little fragments of you
from all the people and places, spaces and times
that split you and splintered pieces of your soul
I am here to remind you
to pull yourself up from the earth
pull your elements back inside
so they can nurture your body
and mend your soul
For you are the earth, my dears
You are fashioned from sacred ground
You are the same
components and compounds
fluids and gases
rhythms and cycles
that form the world beneath your feet
the sky above your head
and all that surrounds you
Your wisdom is earth insight
So listen to the winds and waters
Watch the moon and stars
Stand bare-footed on the land every day
Close your eyes and remember
Do not forget who you are
where you come from
or what you are made of
You are dark muddy soil
wiggling worms and deep roots
delicate blossoms and unfurling leaves
Tread lightly on your own precious soil
Be gentle with yourself and others
Practice the art of conservation
Preserve things of value
within yourself and in your world

do not believe them when they tell you
the earth needs saving
she is not a coin in your pocket
or a bird with a broken wing
She is resilient and robust
A force beyond your understanding
A regenerative power unto herself
It is you who need healing
You who need saving
She is waiting for you to remember
Salvation lies in your balance
So poise yourselves and restore your souls
the world will recover when you do
Save yourselves my darlings
and the world will be saved in turn

c. 2004

We Circle

As women we come together in a circle
We weave our tales of woundings into a cloak of love and hope
We sing songs of healing, chant prayers of peace
Through each other's eyes we see our world as whole
As women we come together in a circle
We share our shadowed dreams and illuminated visions
We dance the rhythms of our hearts to the mother drum
And fan the world soul fire with our consecrated breath
As women we come together in a circle
We wrap our lips around words as lovers of truth
We join hands as bridges of change across the vast expanse of lies
And open our trust gates wide like flowers to the sun

c. 2000

History/Herstory Reprise

He who destroys is not the root
He is simply a stem blighting
a branch of history in decline
Sprung from perplexing displays
of growth, preservation, decay
that precede him
holder of history of The Before,
carrier of pain and suffering
sucked from the soil of time
he too is an outcome

My roots connect to her
the punished, the sufferer
exiled into silence
a vital force pushed under ground
growing in damp darkness
rumbling with life pulsing
outward through centuries
echoing through time
I hear her voice calling
Building strength
Potency pushing through
Thrusting out into the world
Sturdy and wizened
Pain, beauty, healing
Storied in her rings
A cross section of herstory
The sustainer sprung forth

c. 2007

Spring

It's spring again
The slow sleep of winter begins to lift
Soft forest music teases the moon
The seeds of sunrise begin to take root
Preparing for the full bloom of summer
Faint winds blow open
Dormant thoughts awakening
Ideas blossom into actions
As the year waxes warm
The wheel gently turns
The lifeblood quickens
And the newly conceived grows
Within the shielding womb
Tiny buds open shyly
to the welcoming sun
Birds whistle to the hum of bees
The woodlands abuzz with harmony
Passions and desires astir
In fugitive moments of affection
The adoring young maiden returns
The fiery sun rests in a blanket of orange
Against the shadowed silhouette of trees
A choir of crickets ushers in the night
Which wraps itself tenderly around us
And lulls us into springtime dreams

c. 1993

Spring-2

I hide myself
Like a caterpillar
In her cocoon
Weaving my fears
Into a fortress
Enclosing me into
a chrysalis state
I bury the seeds
Of my dreams
Deep beneath
I nourish them
Off my tears
And shelter them
From all that
Would threaten
Their growth
I may appear to be
Dormant
To all external
To myself but inside
Great things
Are germinating
In this very moment
Inside
Profound transformations
Are taking place
Do not be fooled
By that which
Cannot be seen
For my seeds are sprouting
Underground
My wings are nearly complete
I will soon be
Expanding outward
To join you in the garden
Just in time
For spring

c. 1998

Fly on the Wall

I find myself thinking
Then I find myself quiet
Then my tears start to fall
I have learned to be present
And here in the present
I feel like a fly on the wall
I can see my reflection
In the world as it passes
Yet I feel removed from it all
I sense the moonlight upon me
See the starlight within me
I hear my own soul when it calls
I can touch upon silence
But within my own stillness
A deeper sadness remains
I am praising each moment
Feel the life force within me
Breathe out the darkness and pain
I'm observing my judgments
Letting go of attachments
Trying to keep myself real
Still afraid of my shadow
Not sure where I am going
Yet accepting I feel how I feel
I start to feel closer
Then I seem to fall farther
Until I can't tell near from far
I think that none of it matters
I think it all is important
I find all of it truly bizarre
I know nothing's forever
I know everything changes
We just have to be where we are
I come back into silence
Listen to my own heart beat
Close my eyes as I breathe
Aware of my choices
I feel the Earth's pulse below me
Mindful of what I will leave

Is this all my own choosing?
Is this my creation?
A life I've unconsciously made?
With my soul as my compass
I stop on the horizon
Examining each brick I have laid
I catch glimpses of oneness
I get inspired by beauty
I feel love surround me each day
I am grateful for living
I see god all around me
I seize hope as it flutters my way
I'm getting used to not knowing
Try not to guess at what's coming
Watchful my mind doesn't stray
I get stuck in the questions
Until I surrender
And let all that has passed fade away

c. 2008

Eclipse Season

It's eclipse season. My life is getting a shake-up and I'm hearing the
wake-up calls.
No more snooze button schmoozing, avoiding or being insincere.
Time to wake up and take up my place in the game.
Claim my space and say my name loudly, stand proudly amidst the ashes
of shame, the debris of my life that I sent up in flames hoping to reclaim
my dignity.
Time to forget the times I felt so itty bitty tiny worthless, like I was
worth less than a penny, worth less than a skinny chicken.
All bones no meat. A beast not fit for eating or inviting to the feast as a
mere snack.
Time to step away from a life that smacks with defeat and cold feet in
the face of standards no one could possibly meet, standards so pie-in-
the-sky high that the boldest would stumble as the callous cold throngs
rumble in judgment.
Judging a performance that is almost, but not quite, not nearly up to
snuff. A crowd so hard to please that nothing can appease them but the
slow death of a coward in the dust, broadcast in hi-def and they watch as
their own best efforts crumble around them like cheesy crunchy cracker
crumbs that scatter on their cushy couch-y lives.
It's not right.
But it's the way it goes.
It's the way this world gets down and sometimes it gets me down,
crushes my little seedlings of hope, tramples my flowerbed of dreams
and sometimes it seems like the best way to cope is to hang my schemes
by a rope before somebody else does it for me.
Because you see, this world can be inhospitable to change Instead of
rearranging our schedules to accommodate the strange and unusual,
we chain our doors shut and return to our pre-arranged business.
We reclaim our rigid boundaries with self-contained pleasure unable to
measure the losses we've just engendered with our closed off
untouchable life agendas.
It's no wonder I shrink back fearing attack, fearing all eyes on me,
fingers pointing, voices shouting: stop that traitor!
All the haters and debators, stuck in their heads, afraid of their hearts,
too smart for me litigators.
They would rather rip me apart, pick me apart before they even start
listening to what I have to say, to what I try my best to express but
sometimes fall short of articulating clearly.

They only hear the mess up, the less than clear confessions
and I am reduced to merely another dearly pathetic betrayer,
sayer of the things everybody knows but nobody wants to hear.
Not even me.
None-the-less, if I were to guess and then truly confess my best estimate
of this sometimes grueling life test I'd have to say it's something like
this:
something like standing up, speaking up, speaking my truth, my whole
truth, all sides of my story;
standing in my glory and my shame, without blame or apologies;
something like just being who I am no matter what kind of jam this puts
me in or what kind of situation I may later have to back track my way
out of and in the process face the parts of me I'm really not proud of;
just allowing myself to be an entirely human, imperfect, dichotomous,
humbled and bowed, self-aware, self-expressive
face in the crowd.

c. 2011

The Journey

One by one we leave
the sacred circle in silence
to wander alone with our prayers
Weaving patterns in stream beds
And on comet tails
Trailing our wounds behind us
On silver strings of memory
The visioning rites begin
We again find ourselves
Rising and falling
Expanding beyond the constant
drum beat of the heart
Searching for home and hearth
In the opening and closing
We endure peace and loss
Our feet embossing the land
We feel marked and chosen
Beyond our ability to choose
Wearing scars and flowers
Woven loosely around the hours spent
Circling and prowling the truth
As we ascend and descend
Howling at the moon from
the mountain's regal rooftop
Picking up storylines
Like pebbles in our pockets
Scattering our bones
To gather them once again
We dream-walk through sunrise
And past twilight's velvet curtain
We go alone to the sacred river
And endure the threshing-hold
We behold insights and visions
To mold and hold sacred
and return to yearning figures
of illumination and shade
made whole in the water
restored in earth's womb
to rebirth a sense purpose

beyond the entombing self
and we're helped to move
into new arenas with
renewed revelations and
take up new stations
beyond current limitations
and worldly things
as the golden mend rings us
and sings us back into wholeness
we wind our way onward
to the heart of beginnings
and back around to the end
returning time and again
to our mysterious origins

c. 2011

The Long Way

I have been
Scared child crouching
in the basement corner
Invisi-girl in my
moon-silver cape
Trying to escape my nemesis
I have been
Strung out punk
Junkie street girl
Sleeping in bushes
Curls tangled
Locks picked
Hoping to be left alone
I have been bone chilled frozen
Bare foot scalded
By wicked man-serpents
And would-be sister snakes
Slithering around my ankles
Trying to crack my foundation
Back me into a corner
Knife to throat
I have been
On my knees in puddled rain
Hoping to regain a shred of self
I have been
Shelf gathering dust
Rusting from neglect
Left on the side of the road
Far from no home
Alone in paradise
I have been
Prostrate at the feet of ancient deities
Unfolding tea leaves
Scratching symbols into stone
Rubbing skin to earth
Swollen with the future
Suckling gods upon my breast
While being tested to my limits
I have been

Trained in the art of war
Swearing oaths to uphold peace
And to keep the beast at bay
While reciting my *magnum opus*
To those who don't speak Latin
And it just so happens
That I recently climbed the staircase
To find no one there up top
The throne room bare
So I stared out alone into the
Great big empty
slate of my potential
scrolled upon by fate
before I even arrived
So I took up residence
And started my own little hive
Because I've always loved honey

c. 2009

The angels and demons, the fairies and fiends are inside each of us.
It is we who bring them out into the world.
We breathe our life into them and give them form.
It is we who create the hells and heavens,
the pain and the ecstasy here on Earth.
The battle between light and dark, between good and evil,
is within us all.
The internal drama plays itself out on the world stage
and we harm and heal, hate and love, accordingly.

c. 2008

ABOUT THE AUTHOR

Tina Azaria holds a BA in Fine Art and an MA in Depth Psychology and is interested in the healing and integrating potential of the arts. She is an artist, writer, and educator specializing in painting, mask-making, poetry, and performance art. Her creative work addresses the archetypal patterns of Trickster and Shaman, and evokes the potency found in transitions and liminal states. Raised within oral storytelling traditions, she merges story with the creative power of the arts, bridging the realms of consciousness and unconsciousness to unlock the wisdom inherent in the in-between. Tina is owner/founder of Alembic Arts, a multi-modal healing practice in Northern California, where she lives with her husband and two sons. To learn more about Tina and her work visit www.alembicarts.com

www.ingramcontent.com/pod-product-compliance
Lightning Source LLC
Chambersburg PA
CBHW071435090426
42737CB00011B/1665